11-08

D1416730

THE GREAT
HISPANIC HERITAGE

José Martí

THE GREAT HISPANIC HERITAGE

Isabel Allende

Miguel de Cervantes

César Chávez

Salvador Dalí

Gabriel García Márquez

Dolores Huerta

Frida Kahlo

José Martí

Pedro Martinez

Ellen Ochoa

Pablo Picasso

Juan Ponce de León

Diego Rivera

Carlos Santana

Sammy Sosa

Pancho Villa

THE GREAT
HISPANIC HERITAGE

José Martí

Jon Sterngass

CHELSEA HOUSE
PUBLISHERS
An imprint of Infobase Publishing

José Martí

Chelsea House
An imprint of Infobase Publishing
132 West 31st Street
New York NY 10001

Library of Congress Cataloging-in-Publication Data

Sterngass, Jon.
    José Martí / Jon Sterngass.
        p. cm. — (Great Hispanic heritage)
    Includes bibliographical references and index.
    ISBN 0-7910-8841-3 (hardcover)
    1. Martí, José, 1853-1895—Juvenile literature. 2. Cuba—History
—1878-1895—Juvenile literature. 3. Revolutionaries—Cuba—Biography
—Juvenile literature. 4. Statesmen—Cuba—Biography—Juvenile literature. I. Title.
F1783.M38S84 2006
972.91'05092—dc22
                                     [B]

Series design by Terry Mallon/Keith Trego
Cover design by Keith Trego

Printed in the United States of America

Bang EJB 10 9 8 7 6 5 4 3 2 1

This book is printed on acid-free paper.

All links and Web addresses were checked and verified to be correct at the time of publication. Because of the dynamic nature of the Web, some addresses and links may have changed since publication and may no longer be valid.

Table of Contents

1

A Man of Action

Most people's lives are influenced by their childhood experiences. This was especially true for José Martí. Martí's drive to improve the world and help the oppressed can be traced to events that happened to him before he was 18 years old. Early in life, Martí found that he naturally supported the underdog. He grew up to be not only a brilliant poet but also a leader in the fight for "Cuba Libre," a free and independent Cuba.

José Julían Martí y Pérez was born on January 28, 1853, in a small two-story house on Paula Street in Havana, Cuba. José was the oldest brother to seven sisters, two of whom died at a young age. His father, Mariano Martí y Navarro, came from Spain to the Spanish colony of Cuba as a sergeant with the Spanish Army in 1850. Mariano married a girl from the Canary Islands, Leonor Pérez y Cabera. When José was four years old, his family moved from Cuba to Valencia, Spain. Two years later, they returned to the

As a child, José Martí saw slaves working on plantations like this one in Cuba, and at an early age he became aware of how slaveholders treated their property. This cruelty toward slaves drove Martí to defend the powerless later in his life.

island in one of the last waves of colonial emigration. This time they decided to remain in Cuba in the hope of finding a better life.

Largely uneducated, José's parents usually lived on the edge of poverty. Mariano eventually found work with the police force and then served as a night watchman in Havana and other cities in Cuba. The Martí family was not very well off and José had to work from an early age to help the family. When José was only nine, his father took him to the town of Hanábana in the province of Matanzas in western Cuba. There, Mariano allowed José to work as his clerk. The smart boy made an excellent secretary. Mariano began to hope that José could build a career in some white-collar job.

Cuba under Spanish rule was a multiracial society. All shades of skin color, from the lightest to the darkest, could be found in the colony. Slaves, however, were at the bottom of Cuban society, even though they made up more than one-third of Cuba's population. These unfortunate people, usually of African descent, were treated as property by their masters, as if they were a horse or a mule. Their owners thought the slaves' only purpose was to provide free labor for the benefit of their owners. Slaves had no rights or freedoms. In 1860, Cuba had 1,365 sugar mills producing 450,000 tons of sugar a year, almost one-third of the world's supply. In that year, there were about 370,000 slaves in Cuba. Four out of every five slaves worked on the sugar plantations.

In Hanábana, nine-year-old José first saw the brutal treatment of black slaves by landowners and overseers on nearby plantations. José was shocked and extremely upset. As a grown man, he later wrote, "And the blacks? Who has ever seen a friend physically whipped and does not consider himself forever in that man's debt? I saw it, I saw it when I was a child, and I can still feel the shame burning on my cheeks."[1]

The image stayed with Martí throughout his life. He later wrote a poem about his outrage after witnessing the abuse of slaves for the first time when he was a child. He described a scene where the sun rose on a dead slave who had been hanged from a tree:

A small boy witnessed it. He trembled
With feeling for the groaning men,
And at the victim's feet he vowed,
To cleanse the crime with his life.[2]

José Martí traced his desire to fight for freedom and equality directly to that early incident. One of his major concerns was to eliminate slavery and to end racism. Martí was less conscious of people's skin color than almost anyone in Cuba. He would later write, "There is no racial hatred, because there are no races."[3] In another poem, Martí wrote,

> I know of one great sorrow
> Among the nameless ones:
> The world's enormous sorrow
> Is human slavery![4]

The child who witnessed the harsh treatment of African slaves made a decision that would affect the rest of his life. He vowed to side with the powerless against the powerful. In one of his most famous verses, José Martí wrote:

> With the poor of the earth
> I wish to share my fate
> The stream of the mountain
> Pleases me more than the sea.[5]

CUBAN PATRIOT, POET, AND WRITER

José Julián Martí y Pérez grew up to become the brilliant leader of the Cuban independence movement as well as a famous poet and writer. Most people consider him the national hero of Cuba. Martí was a rare combination of a person of ideas and a person of action. He had many talents. He was one of the greatest writers of Spanish America; a founder of Spanish modernist poetry; a persuasive speaker; a teacher of language, literature, and philosophy; a popular journalist; a diplomat; and an organizer of almost every detail of the Cuban war of independence.

The Spanish exiled Martí from Cuba at the age of 17, when he was accused of treason for supporting Cuban independence. He roamed Europe and Latin America for several years

José Martí, depicted in this 1891 oil painting by Herman Norman, encouraged the people of Latin America to be proud of their heritage and to fight for freedom and dignity.

before moving to New York City, where he lived for 15 years. Although Martí worked all his life to free Cuba from Spanish rule, he almost never returned to his homeland.

Martí opposed imperialism in all forms. Imperialism is when one nation controls another nation or territory. While living in New York, Martí sensed that the United States, with all its power and energy, was beginning a selfish program to dominate the Western Hemisphere. He did not want Cuba to win its independence from Spain only to fall under the control of another country, especially the United States. Martí firmly believed that the freedom of Cuba and the Caribbean was necessary for the security of all of Latin America and even the balance of power in the world.

All his life, Martí encouraged the people of Latin America to take pride in their heritage. He proudly proclaimed, "Our patria [country] is one. It begins at the Rio Grande [the border between Mexico and the United States], and it ends in the muddy hills of Patagonia [at the tip of South America]."[6] His most famous essay, entitled "Our America," tried to reveal the underlying unity of all of Hispanic America. He urged cooperation among Latin American nations to turn back the economic and political imperialism of the United States.

In general, Martí could always be found on the side of human freedom and dignity. He supported a fair distribution of wealth to guarantee true social justice in Latin America and the United States. He believed that those who worked the land should own it. Workers should have rights, including the ability to form unions and to strike. Everyone, regardless of wealth or social standing, should receive a good education. Martí always opposed military dictatorship or rule by the army. He believed that the people, through their elected representatives, must make any changes democratically.

José Martí spent almost his entire life as a writer. He produced poetry, political manifestos, speeches, and hundreds of articles and reviews for journals around the world. His collected writings fill more than 25 volumes. More than a century after his death, the life and writings of this revolutionary poet and man of action continue to inspire people throughout the world.

Youth and Exile

The island of Cuba had remained a Spanish colony even when most of Spain's other possessions had broken away. By 1830, countries such as Mexico, Peru, Argentina, Paraguay, Bolivia, Colombia, Venezuela, Chile, and Ecuador had all won their independence. Cuba and Puerto Rico were the last remaining Spanish colonies in the Western Hemisphere, and Spain intended to keep them. In the 1800s, Cuban plantations were the world's most important producers of sugar.

People of Spanish descent who were born and raised in Cuba were known as *criollos* (creoles). Criollos often held managerial positions on sugarcane plantations. However, the Spanish did not allow this Cuban-born "middle class" to take part in governing the prosperous colony. In the middle of the 1800s, many criollos, particularly those in the island's poorer eastern half, known as Oriente, began to complain. They argued that Cubans should be allowed to participate in the Cuban government. Criollos wanted the Spanish government in faraway Madrid to have less control. They com-

In the 1830s, when this depiction of the city of Havana was painted, Cuba was still a colony of Spain. Cuba would not gain its independence from Spain until 1898.

plained that Cubans were being denied the basic rights that Spanish people enjoyed in Spain. Many people living on the island were beginning to feel more Cuban than Spanish. Some people pressed for Cuban independence. Occasionally, criollos even united with the oppressed black slaves who worked the plantations. Almost half a million slaves worked the sugar plantations, more than one-third of the population of Cuba. Needless to say, the slaves had no love for Spanish rule, since the government had brutally put down a series of slave uprisings in the early 1800s.

MARTÍ'S RELATIONSHIP WITH HIS PARENTS

José Martí had a very close relationship with his mother. In his letters, Martí described her as a tender and loving woman. She believed strongly in the power of a good education even though she came from a poor background.

On the other hand, José and his father did not get along. Mariano was strict and stubborn, although he was honest. He remained loyal to Spain for his entire life, working for the Spanish government in Cuba in a variety of positions. In 1880, José wrote to his sister:

> My dear Amelia, you don't know just how much tender respect and veneration our father warrants. While at first he may appear full of grumpiness and silly notions, in fact he's a man with extraordinary virtue. Now that I'm an adult, I can appreciate the value of his energy, as well as the rare, sublime merit of his pure, forthright nature.[7]

As a teenager, however, José was unhappy that his father always seemed to support the Spanish government in Cuba. Mariano simply accepted any wrongs against the Cuban people in the name of Spanish patriotism.

JOSÉ MARTÍ AND RAFAEL MARÍA DE MENDIVE

José Martí's mother insisted that he get an education. She sent him to the San Anacleto School in Havana, where José studied hard and did very well. This success only increased José's problems with his father. Mariano wanted José to quit school and get a paying job as a general clerk or an accountant.

However, his mother got her way. With the help of his godfather, José entered the Escuela Superior Municipal de Varones (Municipal Senior Boys' School) in 1865. The school was directed by Rafael María de Mendive, a Cuban poet and journalist. The Spanish considered Mendive to be very dangerous and perhaps even a traitor. Mendive opposed slavery and supported political independence for Cuba. It was no wonder that Martí idolized Mendive, for Mendive had stated that his goal was "furthering the advancement and improvement of society."[8]

Mendive noticed Martí's talent and became the boy's teacher and advisor. Mendive taught Martí to appreciate poetry and literature. More importantly, he told Martí that he should become aware of social and political injustices in Cuba and take some action against them.

For Martí, Mendive served as a father figure. Mendive gave Martí guidance and affection, and Martí responded in kind. Martí frequently visited the Mendive household. He ate meals there and the Mendives accepted him almost as one of the family. He once wrote to Mendive: "I don't think that a generous father should have to remind his adoring son of his duties . . . when at every moment I would give my life for you—a life which belongs solely to you—and a thousand others if I had them."[9]

THE TEN YEARS' WAR

Mendive had good reason to be upset about the political and social situation in Cuba. By the 1860s, many Cubans were unhappy with their status as a colony of Spain. Spanish taxes were very high. Spanish trade restrictions raised prices and prevented Cuba from developing any crop but sugarcane. Almost no native Cubans held government positions on the island.

In 1865, the Cubans requested tax relief and some minor reforms for the colony. Not only did the Spanish government refuse, but it actually increased taxes in Cuba in 1866 and 1867. Many criollos and middle-class islanders became extremely discouraged with Spanish rule. They concluded that only political independence rather than any surface reforms could help solve their problems.

Cuban dissatisfaction finally boiled over in 1868. People demanded freedom of assembly, freedom of the press, and some representation in the Cortes (the Spanish Parliament). On October 10, Carlos Manuel de Céspedes, a criollo plantation owner who had been involved in uprisings in Spain, began a revolt. Joined by 37 other planters, Céspedes freed his slaves and formed them into a rebel army. He called for Cubans to take up arms and throw out the greedy colonial government. This revolt became known as "*El Grito de Yara*" ("The Cry of

In 1868, Cuban rebels, like the ones depicted here, started an uprising. Known as the Ten Years' War, the conflict was eventually put down by the Spanish in 1878, but it sparked a larger movement that would help Cuba gain its independence from Spain.

Yara") after the small town where the uprising broke out. It began a major movement for Cuban independence from Spain known as the Ten Years' War.

On April 10, 1869, a group of rebels met at Guimaro and adopted a constitution that set up an independent democratic government. Article 24 of the constitution declared, "All the inhabitants of the Republic are absolutely free." The new republic established a capital in Bayamo, a center of revolutionary activity.

There were no major battles between Cuban rebels and the Spanish Army. Instead, the fighting consisted of brutal guerrilla warfare, especially on the eastern part of the island. In the fourth month of the war, Spanish soldiers tried to recapture the rebel city of Bayamo. The inhabitants of the city burned Bayamo to the ground rather than return it to the Spanish, an event that is still recalled in Cuba's national anthem. Céspedes called for the rebels to burn all the sugarcane fields and plantations to make the colony unprofitable and convince the Spanish to leave. About 50,000 Cubans, including Céspedes himself, and more than 200,000 Spanish perished in the Ten Years' War.

As the war dragged on, two revolutionary leaders became especially important. Antonio Maceo, the "Bronze Titan," was the son of a freed slave. He became an expert in the guerrilla warfare waged by the Cubans in the eastern part of the island. Dominican-born Máximo Gómez led the more traditional Cuban revolutionary army. Gómez had been a commander in the Spanish Army. In the Ten Years' War, he enlisted with Céspedes as a sergeant and rose through the ranks to become an outstanding leader. Although these two heroes would not be victorious in the Ten Years' War, both men would remain important in the independence movement. They would also both play a crucial role in the life of José Martí.

DEFENDING THE PATRIA

Although he was only 15 years old when the Ten Years' War began, Martí wholeheartedly supported the revolt against Spain. With Mendive's help, Martí wrote articles for the underground newspapers that suddenly appeared throughout Havana. He worked for independence with Fermín Valdés Domínguez, another of Mendive's students. Martí and Domínguez would turn out to be lifelong friends.

In January 1869, José Martí published pamphlets called *El Diablo Conjuelo* (*The Limping Devil*) and *La Patria Libre* (*The Free Homeland*). Martí praised the Cuban war of independence and the revolutionary fighters. In *La Patria Libre*, Martí included a long dramatic poem in eight scenes called "Abdala." Abdala, the hero of the poem, decides to defend his *patria* with his life against the advice of his mother. In the moment of victory, Abdala is killed fighting for his country. The play ends with Martí's hero saying, "I die happy; death matters little to me. . . . Oh, how sweet it is to die, when I die fighting boldly to defend my patria!"[10] Throughout his life, Martí expressed a desire to die a martyr's death for Cuba. (A martyr is a person who chooses to suffer death or torture rather than give up his or her beliefs or cause.)

THE *VIRGINIUS* AFFAIR (1873)

During the Ten Years' War, Cuban exiles in the United States held mass meetings, produced propaganda, and organized expeditions to help the rebels. The U.S. government wanted to extend its power into the Caribbean Sea but did not want to fight a war with Spain to do it. Some North Americans, however, felt an obligation to help the Cubans, whom they considered freedom fighters.

The *Virginius* was a Cuban-owned vessel that had been fraudulently flying the American flag for years while it illegally carried weapons and supplies from the United States to Cuban rebels. On October 31, 1873, a Spanish warship captured the *Virginius*. After hasty, secret court-martials in Santiago, Cuba, the Spanish executed Captain Joseph Fry and 52 crewmembers and passengers. Some of those who were executed were citizens of Great Britain and the United States.

This insult to the flag caused an outburst of patriotism in the United States. Americans held protests from Boston to New Orleans. The U.S. ambassador to Spain made the situation worse with his bluster and the Spanish barely prevented a mob from attacking U.S. citizens in Spain. The U.S. government demanded an apology and a large payment for damages within 12 days. War between the United States and Spain seemed very likely.

However, when the U.S. government learned the truth about the *Virginius*, it softened its demands. After several days, a settlement was reached. Spain gave the United States $80,000 for the families of the executed Americans. For the rest of his life, José Martí considered Captain Fry a hero and a martyr to the cause of Cuban independence.

Martí used the Spanish word patria a great deal. It is a difficult word to translate into English. Martí's patria meant more than just "country" or "homeland." A person belonged to a patria as a matter of choice. After all, Máximo Gómez had not been born in Cuba, and Martí himself would spend less than half of his life there. To Martí, a patriot supported a patria absolutely but not blindly. The patria required selfless commitment and sacrifice, but a person never defended it if it was in the wrong. Martí would spend his entire life expanding on or explaining this difficult concept.

ARREST

In January 1869, a riot broke out in a theater in Havana. Spanish soldiers stormed the building, arresting many of the spectators and killing members of the unarmed crowd. Neither Mendive nor Martí was at the performance but the Spanish authorities felt it was important to set an example. Therefore, they arrested Mendive and threw him in prison. At great personal risk, Martí visited Mendive during his five-month sentence. He also helped take care of Mendive's family and assisted in the running of his school. The Spanish banished Mendive from Cuba in 1869. Soon Martí would find himself caught in the same web.

On October 21, 1869, Spanish authorities arrested Martí and his friend Fermín Valdés Domínguez for possessing writings that supported the revolution. These "writings" were actually nothing more than a single letter criticizing a fellow student's selfishness and thoughtlessness for joining the Spanish side. The two friends had written it but had not sent it or published it. Unfortunately, neither of them had thought to destroy the letter. As a result, they were charged with treason.

The two boys spent more than four months in a Havana jail before they were finally court-martialed. Martí wrote to his mother: "I am sorry to be behind bars, but my imprisonment is very useful to me. It has given me plenty of lessons for my life, which I foresee will be short."[11]

On March 4, 1870, Valdés Domínguez received a sentence of six months in prison. Martí, however, accepted full responsibility for the letter and took a bold and rebellious attitude toward the court. Although he was only 17 years old, the court sentenced Martí to six years of hard labor in the Havana stone quarries.

IMPRISONMENT AND EXILE

José Martí spent six months in the San Lázaro stone quarries of Havana performing backbreaking work splitting rocks. He wore an iron waist-chain and leg shackles that the guards never removed. The chains on his feet permanently scarred his ankles. The work left him a physical wreck, half-blind from his labor in the tropical sun. A blow from a guard with a chain caused a hernia that bothered Martí for the rest of his life. The experience in prison left a lasting impression on him. After his release, Martí carried around a ring made from a link of the chain that he had worn in prison. Inside the ring, Martí engraved the word *Cuba*.

Martí's family feared he would die if he stayed in the stone quarries much longer. Friends of Mariano Martí's from the army managed to have José's punishment reduced to a lighter sentence. The Spanish authorities in Cuba transferred José Martí to a regular prison on the Isle of Pines and pardoned him in January 1871. However, the Spanish feared he would again become involved in revolutionary activities in Cuba. To prevent this, they exiled him to Spain. The Spanish government in Cuba often dealt with so-called troublemakers in this way.

Martí never forgot the horrifying six months of his imprisonment. More than 10 years later, Martí published a collection of poems that included his recollections of prison life. He wrote: "Yes! I too, my head shorn, my ankles bound with heavy chain. . . . And I am still appalled to see in memory what once my eyes did see. And terrified, I rise to my feet as if to venture an escape! Some memories sear the mind!"[12]

Even though he was out of the quarries, Martí was still upset that he would have to leave Cuba. He wrote Mendive a farewell letter that expressed his devotion to his teacher: "In two hours I will be deported to Spain. I have suffered much but feel that I have suffered well. If I have been strong enough to meet this and if I am able to be a true man, this is all due to you. Indeed, all the warmth and kindness I have is due solely to you."[13] Martí left his family and his homeland for Spain on January 15, 1871. He would see Cuba again for only two brief periods until he came back to fight for its freedom in 1895.

At age 18, many of Martí's basic character traits were already set. His relationship with his closed-minded father and the energetic Rafael Mendive affected his vision of the world. The brutal imprisonment he suffered hardened his desire to change the situation in Cuba. Martí later wrote a simple explanation to Máximo Gómez about how his career as a professional revolutionary began: "Rafael Mendive was my father; from his school I went to jail and then to political prison; then I was deported."[14] For the rest of his life, Martí would be a political exile and a fighter for the independence of Cuba.

3

A Life
of Travel

José Martí found that there are certainly worse punishments in life than to be forced to go to Madrid as a young man. Martí quickly found work as a tutor to a wealthy family. He enrolled in the University of Madrid and later at the University of Zaragoza. Martí mainly studied law and philosophy but he read tirelessly. He investigated everything from modern scientific journals to Hindu mythology, from Spanish classics to British drama. He met with literary groups, visited art galleries, and frequently went to the theater.

Martí also continued to work for change in Cuba. Immediately after arriving in Madrid, he wrote *El presido político en Cuba* (*The Political Prison in Cuba*). This pamphlet harshly criticized the brutal treatment of political prisoners in Cuba by the Spanish government. Martí's writings quickly attracted attention in Spain even though the author was only 18 years old. The Ten Years' War had made people in Spain interested in a firsthand account of what was going on in their colonies in the Caribbean. Spanish readers liked

As a young man, José Martí traveled to Madrid, Spain (pictured here), where he attended college and enjoyed the cultural attractions of the city.

Martí's vigorous writing style, and newspapers asked him to write regularly about the situation in Cuba. Martí met other Cuban exiles living in Madrid who were excited by his fiery speeches. He was now almost as involved in Cuban politics as he could have been if he were living in Cuba.

THE 27 OF NOVEMBER

Although Martí supported Cuban independence from Spain, he had not totally given up on the possibility that Cuba could exist peacefully as part of the Spanish Empire. However, a shocking incident in Cuba changed Martí's view.

On November 27, 1871, pro-Spanish volunteers seized a group of medical students from the University of Havana. According to the Spanish authorities in Cuba, the students had been disrespectful to the grave of Gonzalo Castañón. (Castañón was a pro-Spanish newspaper editor who had been assassinated in the United States by Cuban rebels.) Eight of the students were condemned to death and shot at 4:00 A.M., on the same morning as their arrest. The government sentenced 30 other people to work on chain gangs for four to six years.

People throughout the world condemned the actions of the Spanish government. The incident brought new support for the Cuban rebels in the Ten Years' War. Martí was particularly shocked. The bloody incident convinced him that the Spanish colonial system was hopelessly unjust. He would no longer accept anything less than complete independence for Cuba.

Fermín Valdés Domínguez had joined Martí in exile. Together, they wrote a pamphlet entitled *The 27 of November*. The work contained a poem written by Martí and dedicated to the eight medical students. In it, Martí called on Cubans everywhere to swear "an oath of infinite love of country . . . over their bodies."[15]

THE SHORT-LIVED FIRST SPANISH REPUBLIC

In 1873, after various uprisings throughout Spain, King Amadeus was forced to give up his throne. Martí was delighted when the first Spanish Republic was established on February 11. He believed that a Spanish nation ruled by representatives elected by the people would not tolerate Spain's brutal colonial policy toward Cuba.

In response to these events, Martí wrote *La Républica Española y la Revolución Cubana* (*The Spanish Republic and the Cuban Revolution*). In it, he argued that if Spain had the right of self-government, then so did Cuba. Unfortunately, Spain's policy toward Cuba did not change in a meaningful way after the republic was established. The new government was afraid of being accused of being "soft" on Cuba and continued the war against the rebels. This foreign policy did not save the government. The First Spanish Republic collapsed in January 1874; it had not even lasted a year. Military revolts and then a brutal civil war followed. The Spanish people adopted a new constitution in 1876, but by then, Martí had left the country.

Martí's sentence of exile stated that he had to remain in Spain. This punishment was relaxed in January 1875. However, the Spanish government still would not permit Martí to return to Cuba. With the Ten Years' War still raging, the Spanish wanted to keep revolutionaries far away from the colony. So, after receiving his degree, Martí briefly visited France and Great Britain and then moved to Mexico. His family had moved there after Martí's exile, and he had not seen them in four years.

CONTENT IN MEXICO

José Martí arrived in the port of Vera Cruz, Mexico, in February 1875 and lived in Mexico for almost two years. He enjoyed his time there and his writing thrived. Martí said that "next to his own [Mexico] was the country he loved most."[16]

As usual, Martí had his hand in many different activities. He seemed to have unlimited energy. Martí mainly earned money writing for newspapers but he also became well known as a public speaker. He participated in political debates at schools. His play, *Amor con Amor se Paga* (*Love Is Repaid by Love*), written for the Spanish actress Concha Padilla, was a hit in Mexico City.

In Mexico, Martí met up with the lawyer Manuel Mercado, a friend of his family. The two became lifelong friends and Martí later dedicated some of his poetry to Mercado. Through the influence of Mercado, Martí published articles in Mexico City's *La Revista Universal* (*The Universal Review*) dealing with art, drama, and social issues. In addition, Martí used the pen name "Orestes" to write poems about Mexico City's cultural life. His fame spread through educated circles in Latin America.

Martí also threw himself into Mexico's political affairs. As usual, Martí could not help but side with the underdog. In January 1876, he represented laborers at an assembly of workers in Chihuahua. In newspaper articles, Martí drew special attention to the problems of Indians in Mexican society. Martí wrote, "Until the Indian is allowed to go forward, America will not begin to advance." Of course, Martí also worked for the cause of Cuban independence. He raised funds for the revolutionary movement and dreamed about returning home. He felt like a citizen of Mexico, yet he never lost any of his pride in being Cuban.

RETURN TO CUBA

In 1876, Porfirio Díaz staged a military coup and took over the Mexican presidency from Sebastián Lerdo de Tejada. Martí had admired and supported Tejada. The disappointed Martí condemned Díaz as self-serving and corrupt. Martí decided it was time to leave Mexico. He told a friend that he had been extremely content there but could not stay in good conscience with Díaz as president. He wrote, "For anyone with a beam of light on their brow, it is not possible to live where tyrants rule."[17] He would later leave Guatemala and then Venezuela for the same reason. For the rest of his life, Martí distrusted military leaders who pledged to support democracy. This suspicion would greatly affect his relationship with Cuban generals Antonio Maceo and Máximo Gómez.

Martí decided to take a chance and return illegally to Cuba in January 1877. After he arrived, he traveled around under a false name—Julián Peréz—that combined his middle name and his mother's maiden name. Martí spent a month in Cuba without anyone recognizing him but he could not find any decent work without being identified.

Martí also saw no immediate hope for the cause of Cuban independence. The rebels had suffered heavy losses in the Ten Years' War. The countryside suffered from the destruction caused by constant guerrilla warfare. Spain taxed Cuba heavily to pay for the war and this had damaged the economy. Martí was depressed. He believed that a successful revolution was impossible at the time. He decided that he could do more for the cause of Cuban independence overseas than in Cuba.

José Martí left Mexico soon after the rise to power of President Porfirio Díaz, whom he considered corrupt. Díaz is pictured here in an 1870 photo.

GUATEMALA

After leaving Cuba, Martí settled in Guatemala in March 1877. He was lucky that Guatemala's president, Justo Rufino Barrios, had appointed a distinguished Cuban, José María Izaguirre, as director of the Central School. Like Martí, Izaguirre supported Cuban independence. He knew Martí could speak French and English and knew Latin and Greek. Izaguirre hired Martí to teach literature, philosophy, and history at the school.

Martí loved Guatemala. He wrote that the country possessed "wide roads, natural splendors, a big-hearted character, a benevolent government, an eagerness for betterment and riches . . . a delightful climate, [and] picturesque villages."[18]

In addition to teaching, Martí kept busy as usual. He lectured, founded cultural clubs, helped edit a journal called the *Revista de la Universidad*, wrote articles on Guatemala's new legal code, and published a history of Guatemala. He also wrote a play called *Drama Indio* and one of his most famous poems, "*La Niña de Guatemala*" ("The Young Woman of Guatemala").

At first, Martí admired President Barrios. He especially liked Barrios's attempt to curb the power of the Roman Catholic Church. Barrios had replaced the Catholic schools and universities in Guatemala with secular (nonreligious) ones. However, Barrios was also a dictator who did not allow any opposition to his rule. Slowly, Guatemala's political environment began to change. Barrios began to rely on brute force to rule the country. Martí did not like the change and began to think about leaving Guatemala. On April 6, 1878, Martí resigned his position when Barrios unfairly dismissed Izaguirre as director of the school. But where would he go?

THE LITTLE WAR AND SECOND EXILE

In 1878, the Ten Years' War between Spain and Cuba finally ended. Spanish General Arsenio Martínez de Campos helped write the Pact (Treaty) of Zanjón, which officially ended the Ten Years' War. This agreement promised political reforms for Cuba and gave the colony some representation in the Spanish government. As part of the treaty, Spain declared that all Cubans who had been convicted of political crimes would be granted a complete pardon.

Martí decided to take advantage of the pardon and return to Cuba. He tried to practice law in Cuba but could not get a license because of his past prison record. Instead, he worked in a law office in Havana and continued his political activities and writings against Spanish rule.

Unfortunately, the Spanish government broke almost all the promises in the Pact of Zanjón (although the government did abolish slavery in 1886). There was tremendous discontent in Cuba when conditions did not improve. The Cuban economy suffered because of the destruction of so many sugar plantations. Martí was both disappointed and angry. He spoke out publicly, announcing that he believed independence was the solution to Cuban problems. He began to refer to Cuba as "our nation." "Rights," he declared, were "to be taken, not requested; seized, not begged for."[19]

On August 26, 1879, hundreds of farmers and slaves attacked the Spanish stronghold in Santiago. Riots and demonstrations against the government broke out throughout Cuba. This was the beginning of *La Guerra Chiquita* (The Little War) for Cuban independence. The Spanish colonial government decided to prevent any further uprisings by restricting freedom of speech, the press, and assembly. Ramón Blanco, the Spanish governor, called Martí "a dangerous madman" and called for his immediate imprisonment.[20] However, Martí still had powerful friends and they tried to help him. They managed to get Blanco to promise that he would not bring Martí to trial if Martí publicly gave up his revolutionary views and declared his support for the Spanish colonial government. Martí supposedly replied, "Tell the General that Martí is not the kind of man that can be bought."[21] Under these conditions, the Spanish would not allow Martí to stay in Cuba. He was arrested on September 17, 1879, and briefly imprisoned. A week later, the authorities deported him to Spain for the second time.

At this point, Martí decided that there was no reason to return to Cuba until the time was right for revolution. He would not come home for 16 years. Martí was not alone. Some Cubans fled to other countries and formed the Cuban Revolutionary Committee. This organization, headquartered in New York City, issued a call for all Cubans to work for the cause of independence.

Martí only stayed in Spain for a few months. This time, he simply left the country without asking anyone's permission. After a brief stay in France, Martí sailed for New York. He arrived in January 1880 and found work writing for several New York City newspapers.

The Little War Fails

In May 1880, Calixto García, the head of the New York Cuban Revolutionary Committee, landed in Cuba to lead a new revolt against Spain. Martí, the interim president of the committee, issued a passionate proclamation announcing García's presence in Cuba and urging Cubans to rise up and support him. Over the summer, however, the rebellion crumbled. García surrendered to Spanish troops in August. By October 1880, it was clear that The Little War had also failed. Martí sadly wrote, "Our honor itself, and our very cause, demand that we abandon the field of armed warfare."[22]

General Máximo Gómez retired to the Dominican Republic, although he continued to keep in touch with Cuban affairs. Antonio Maceo went into exile in Mexico. He denounced the Pact of Zanjón and continued to work for Cuban independence even while he was in exile. Some rebels never surrendered and continued fighting in the mountains for the next 17 years. For the moment, the Cuban Revolutionary Committee of New York ceased to exist.

STOPOVER IN VENEZUELA

In 1881, Martí jumped at the offer of a teaching position in Venezuela. He taught there for a few months and even managed to start a magazine called La Revista Venezolana (The Venezuelan Review). However, Martí quarreled with the Venezuelan president, Antonio Guzmán Blanco. Guzmán Blanco had helped Venezuela in many ways but, like Justo Rufino Barrios in Guatemala, he was a dictator. Guzmán Blanco did not allow anyone to criticize him. He filled Venezuela with statues and paintings of himself. In July,

In 1880, Calixto García, the head of the New York Cuban Revolutionary Committee, led a failed rebellion to oust the Spanish from Cuba. However, García would later win a number of victories during the campaign against the Spanish in 1895–96.

Martí angered Guzmán Blanco by writing an article that praised Cecilio Acosta, a Venezuelan writer and poet. The president expected a similar article to be written about him. Martí, with his old distrust of military dictators, decided it would be better if he did not stay. He left Venezuela on July 28, 1881, for the United States. *La Revista Venezolana* lasted for only two issues.

Once again, as in Mexico and Guatemala, Martí's refusal to accept absolute rule had brought him into conflict with the leaders of the country in which he was living. These dictators found it impossible to buy Martí's praise or his silence. Martí's refusal to be intimidated when confronted by injustice won him widespread admiration wherever he lived.

LOVE AND MARRIAGE

While Martí was living in Mexico, he met Carmen Zayas Bazán, the daughter of a wealthy Cuban aristocrat in exile. They were soon engaged to be married. However, when Martí moved to Guatemala, Carmen remained with her family in Mexico.

In Guatemala, Martí became friends with General Miguel García Granado and fell in love with the general's daughter, María. Unfortunately, Martí was still engaged to Carmen at the time. He could have broken off the engagement but decided not to do so. In December 1877, Martí went to Mexico, married Carmen, and brought her back to Guatemala. María became sick and died. According to the official records, María died of tuberculosis, but Martí did not believe it. In her memory, he wrote one of his most famous poems, "La Niña de Guatemala" ("The Young Woman of Guatemala"), about a young lady "who died of love."

In the poem, Martí remembers that María gave him a little pincushion to remember her by when he left her to go to Mexico. The poem ends with her burial:

> At dusk she entered the river;
> The doctor pulled out her body.
> They say she died of cold;
> I know she died of love.[23]

Unlike many romantic works of the time, the narrator (Martí) seems very detached from the tragic death. In this poem, he is more interested in telling the story than revealing

ISMAELILLO

With his son living in Cuba, José Martí felt like a failure as a father. In Venezuela, he wrote *Ismaelillo*, which was published in 1882. *Ismaelillo* was a collection of 15 poems that expressed Martí's love and longing for his son. Nowhere in the poem did he mention any desire to be reunited with his wife. Just before his death, Martí wrote, "None of my verses should be published before *Ismaelillo*. None of them are worth bothering with."*

In *Ismaelillo*, Martí continually gives his son instructions that actually sound more like orders. He tells his son that good behavior is very important. In fact, Martí says that his son is better off dead than living a life of immorality, impurity, and deceit.

However, Martí's desire to be with his son is also symbolic. If the father were with his family in Cuba, that would also mean that Cuba must be free and independent. Then Martí would no longer be exiled from his own country. Yet Martí cannot help but return to the theme of a martyr's death. His desire for Cuba's independence always seems to become confused with his own fascination with self-sacrifice.

> To find you, son,
> I cross the seas.
> The kindly waves
> Take me to you;
> Fresh breezes
> Cleanse my flesh
> Of city
> Worms;
> But I am sad,
> Since on the seas
> I cannot shed my blood
> For anyone.

* José Martí, *Jose Marti, Major Poems: A Bilingual Edition*. Trans. Elinor Randall. Ed. Philip S. Foner (New York: Holmes and Meier, 1982), 6.

his own emotions. Martí's relations with women would be complicated throughout his life.

Martí's son, José Martí Zayas Bazán, was born in Cuba on November 22, 1878. There are many photographs of José Martí but one of the few that shows him with a smile on his face is when he holds his young son in his arms.

Despite his obvious happiness with his son, Martí's marriage did not work out. When he was exiled to Spain for the second time, Carmen stayed in Cuba with 10-month-old José. She did not share her husband's concern with politics. Carmen wanted a quiet, safe life without the constant fear of exile, imprisonment, or worse. Her husband, wrapped up in the cause of Cuban independence, did not put much effort into his family life. Martí later wrote a novel in which the main character and hero seemed to be in a situation resembling his own:

> He traveled because he was full of eagles, which gnawed at his body, and wanted wide spaces, and were suffocating in the prison of the city. He traveled because he was married to a woman whom he thought he had loved, and whom he then found like an insensible cup, in which the harmonies of his soul found no echo.[24]

Carmen came to New York to live with Martí for a while but they kept arguing. In fact, Carmen admitted that she could quite easily live under Spanish rule in Cuba. She did not share her husband's enthusiasm or commitment to start a Cuban revolution. Nor did she like life in New York. In January 1881, she returned to Cuba with little José. Over the next 10 years, Carmen visited her husband in New York three times but stayed only a few months each time before returning to Cuba. Ironically, Carmen raised little José, José Martí's son, to become a strong supporter of Spanish rule of Cuba.

José Martí in New York

José Martí arrived in New York in January 1880. He took a room in a boardinghouse at 51 East 29th Street in Manhattan. Two Cuban emigrants owned and operated the boardinghouse: Manuel Mantilla and his wife, Carmen (Carmita) Miyares de Mantilla.

At first, Martí could not find a steady job. Still, he resumed working for the Cuban independence movement. Martí was respected enough to be named spokesperson and then temporary president of the Cuban Revolutionary Committee. Then, he became friends with Charles Anderson Dana, a wealthy and powerful New York newspaper publisher and editor. Dana invited Martí to contribute to a weekly New York literary magazine called *The Hour*. Martí wrote 29 short essays in *The Hour* in 1880 on a variety of topics, including a famous series on his first impressions of the United States. This writing job led to others, and Martí was soon earning a living in the United States.

In 1880, José Martí moved to New York City (depicted here in a panoramic view from the same time period), where he served as a joint consul for Uruguay, Paraguay, and Argentina. While Martí lived in the United States, he became an influential writer.

As always, Martí had an unbelievable amount of energy. He wrote hundreds of articles and essays for a variety of newspapers, reviews, journals, and magazines. He translated novels, essays, and poetry from Spanish to English and from English to Spanish. He published a magazine for children. His writing made him so admired throughout Spanish-speaking America that the governments of Uruguay, Paraguay, and Argentina appointed him their consul (representative) in New York. He composed some of his best poetry and prose during this period. Except for some short trips to Central and South America, Martí would spend the last 15 years of his life in the United States, mostly in New York.

RELATIONSHIP WITH CARMITA MANTILLA

When Martí moved to New York, he was 27 years old, slightly built, and of medium height. He usually dressed in black suits and a black silk bow tie. His clothes were rarely fancy because he did not have a lot of money, but they were always clean and neat.

Martí had not stayed at the boardinghouse for too long before he fell in love with Carmita Mantilla. Manuel Mantilla, her husband and the father of her three children, was a very sick man. Eleven months after Martí's arrival in New York, Carmita gave birth to María Mantilla (November 28, 1880). Six weeks later, María was baptized at St. Patrick's Church in Brooklyn, New York. Her mother was listed as Carmen Miyares de Mantilla and her father as Manuel Mantilla. José Martí was listed as her godfather, but it seems likely that Martí was actually the baby's father. María's son, the well-known movie actor Cesar Romero, always maintained that José Martí was his grandfather. Romero claimed that Carmita admitted the truth to a friend of hers at the time of Martí's death, although that friend did not tell María that Martí was her father until 1935.

Whether she was his child or not, Martí loved María like a father would. He raised her and referred to her as his daughter. After Manuel Mantilla's death in 1885, Martí became a father figure to all four of Carmita's children. He educated the girls himself, taught them various languages, and encouraged them to become teachers.

For years, Martí lived apart from his wife, Carmen Zayas Bazán, and his son, José. The couple separated permanently after Carmen briefly visited New York in 1890. She returned to Cuba, taking José with her without Martí's consent. He never saw his wife or his son again.

In Carmita, Martí found a constant companion who shared his dreams of an independent Cuba. In 1895, Martí wrote to María: "When someone is nice to me, or nice to Cuba, I show them your picture. My wish is that you all live together, with your mother, and that you have a good life." A few weeks before his death, Martí wrote, "Love your mother. I've never known a better woman in this world. I can't, nor will I ever, think of her without seeing how clear and beautiful life is. Take great care of this treasure."[25]

Actor Cesar Romero, pictured here in 1967, always claimed that José Martí was his biological grandfather. Romero's most famous role was as the Joker in the television series *Batman*, which aired in the late 1960s.

MARTÍ THE JOURNALIST

Martí's main source of income in New York came from his positions at a variety of North American and Latin American newspapers. Martí wrote a number of articles from 1881 to 1883 on life in the United States for *La Opinión Nacional* of Caracas, Venezuela. He also wrote regularly for *El Partido Liberal* of México from 1886 to 1892. These articles were reprinted in many newspapers throughout Latin America. This made Martí one of the first international journalists.

More importantly, Martí was the North American correspondent for *La Nación*, an Argentinean newspaper founded in 1870. His first article for *La Nación*, written in July 1882, dealt with the execution of Charles Guiteau, the assassin of U.S. President James Garfield. His last article, written in March 1891, described Southern mobs lynching Italian immigrants in New Orleans. In between, he wrote on nearly every aspect of life in the United States: news of the day, labor struggles, biographies of leading citizens, descriptions of elections, buildings, prizefights, trials, murders, Valentine's Day, and the activities of high society. He tried to paint a complete picture of the United States as he knew it for his Latin American readers.

Martí also benefited from his relationship with Charles Dana. Dana had bought the *New York Sun* in 1868 and, as editor, he made the newspaper famous for the quality of its articles and editorials. The *Sun* was supposedly the best-written newspaper in the United States during this period. Luckily for Martí, Dana was obsessed with the struggle for freedom in Cuba. The *New York Sun* was the most important newspaper supporting Cuban independence. Dana became a close friend of Martí's and gave him both a way to make a living and a platform from which to argue for Cuban independence.

At first glance, Martí's stories about life in the United States appear to be written in the wordy style that most nineteenth-century readers enjoyed. However, Martí adopted a remarkable and unmistakable technique. His "Letters from New York" often switch topics very quickly. These articles could make the reader dizzy by combining many different perspectives and images in one essay, sometimes even in a single sentence. Martí's unique writing style mixed fact and poetry, the personal and political, the heroic and the everyday. His articles and essays often swept the reader off his or her feet, but sometimes made people throw down the newspaper in frustration.

For example, Martí wrote one of his most famous articles in 1881 on Coney Island. This was a part of New York, "four years ago an abandoned sand bank, that today is a spacious amusement area." Here is just one sentence from Martí's essay, published in the newspaper *La Pluma* in Bogotá, Colombia:

> The amazing thing there is the size, the quantity, the sudden tangible outcropping of human activity, this sudden result of human activity, this immense valve of pleasure opened to an immense people, these dining rooms that, seen from afar, look like the encampments of armies, these roads that from two miles away are not roads at all but long carpets of heads, the daily surge of a prodigious people onto a prodigious beach, that mobility, that faculty for progress, this enterprise, this altered form, this fevered rivalry in wealth, the monumentality of the whole, which makes this seaside resort comparable in majesty to the earth that bears it, the sea that caresses it, and the sky that crowns it, this rising tide, this overwhelming and invincible, constant and frenetic drive to expand, and taking for granted of these very wonders—that is the amazing thing here.[26]

Obviously, not all of Martí's sentences are this long. However, he did strive for mood and literary effect even as he tried to inform Latin Americans about life in the United States in the so-called Gilded Age (1876–1900). He wrote these sketches for 10 years in New York. Collected together, they fill five thick books. Martí based some of his sketches on personal experience, such as one he wrote on New York's Great Blizzard of 1888. Other articles, such as the burning of a black man at the stake in Texarkana, Texas, Martí based on reports he read in other New York newspapers. In all cases, he wrote about life in America from the unique perspective of a Cuban stranded in a culture that was not his own.

THE TRANSLATOR

While in the United States, Martí also earned money by translating books back and forth between Spanish, French, and English. For a while, he worked for D. Appleton and Company, a famous publisher in New York City. Probably his most famous work of translation was *Ramona*, a novel by Helen Hunt Jackson. Jackson was famous in her time for her attempts to help Native Americans and defend them against racism. Martí admired her writing and politics a great deal and translated *Ramona* into Spanish in 1884, the same year it was published in English. Martí also translated textbooks on agriculture, logic, and ancient history.

Translating was a good way for Martí to sharpen his own writing skills. The act of translation forced him to consider the meaning and use of every word carefully. When Martí translated the French novelist Victor Hugo's *Mes Fils* (*My Sons*) from French into Spanish, Martí wrote, "Victor Hugo does not write in French and he cannot be translated into Spanish. Victor Hugo writes in Victor Hugo, and what a difficult thing it is to translate him!"[27]

LA AMÉRICA

One of Martí's constant worries was that people in South America and the Caribbean did not really understand the United States. In June 1883, Martí took a job as editor of *La América*, a magazine with offices at 756 Broadway in New York City. *La América* claimed that it was a magazine of "Agriculture, Industry, and Commerce" for general readers. However, Martí became the editor in chief when the ownership of *La América* changed in December of that year. He had very specific goals. On his promotion, he said he wanted "to explain the mind of the United States of the North to the minds of those who are in spirit and will someday be in form, the United States of South America."[28] He later wrote in the magazine, "Our greatest desire is to bring together the souls and the hands of our Latin American peoples."[29]

Martí wrote articles for *La América* on an amazingly wide range of topics, including Native American art, U.S. trade policy, and graduation day at a women's college. Typical of Martí's work for *La América* is his detailed report on the opening of the Brooklyn Bridge, the longest suspension bridge in the world at the time. Martí mixed precise statistics on the weight of the bridge and the length of the cables with a grand analysis of the meaning of the moment. He wrote:

> On May 24, 1883, the bridge was opened to the public . . . along which a hundred thousand men, packed together and panting, now rush from dawn to midnight. Watching this vast, well-scrubbed, teeming, and ever-growing multitude gather to swarm rapidly across this airborne tendril, you can imagine that you are seeing Liberty herself seated on high . . . Liberty who has given birth to this daughter in this city. Liberty who is the mother of the new world that is only now dawning. It is as if the sun were rising over these two towers.[30]

MARTÍ AND RELIGION

In 1889, Martí began yet another new project. He started a new magazine for "the children of America" called *La Edad de Oro* (*The Golden Age*). Martí edited the magazine and, as usual, contributed some of the articles. *La Edad de Oro* contained a wide range of stories, poems, fairy tales, and nonfiction articles on topics like children's games or travels in Vietnam. Martí had always been interested in children's education and this was one of the first examples of children's literature in Latin America. *La Edad de Oro* only lasted for four issues. The magazine's financial backer was a wealthy Brazilian who withdrew his funding, because Martí refused to mention God or religion in the children's magazine.

Although Martí was a Catholic by birth, he never thought very highly of the religion. He once wrote, "I want to educate my nation so that they will save anyone who is drowning and will never go to Mass."[31] Martí was particularly angry at the

José Martí thought the Catholic Church was partly responsible for keeping Cuba under the control of Spain. Despite his feelings toward the Church, Martí is buried at the José Cementerio Santa Efigenia, which is near the Catholic cathedral of Santiago de Cuba (pictured here).

role of the Roman Catholic Church in Cuba. He believed that most of the priests sided with the Spanish government. He thought it was almost treasonous to preach that the people should passively accept Spanish tyranny and hope for a better life in the next world. Martí's vision was for a secular Cuba with the Catholic Church stripped of all its power and political influence. He especially opposed religious education in the Cuban school system.

Even in New York, Martí wrote several articles complaining about the Catholic Church's meddling in political issues. He became very angry when a Catholic priest in New York was punished for supporting a candidate for mayor who was not the same one chosen by the archbishop of New York. Martí later wrote, "I think that the idea of priests getting involved in politics . . . is the worst form of stealing. It is akin [similar] to an illegal seizure of the faithfuls' souls."[32]

SUPPORT FOR CUBAN INDEPENDENCE

Despite all his other projects, Martí spent most of his time in New York working for Cuban independence. He spoke at countless meetings for the cause of Cuba Libre. He poured out a stream of essays, articles, and pamphlets supporting the Cuban revolutionary cause. After the defeat of the Cuban revolutionaries in The Little War in 1880, Martí played an important role in boosting the spirits of Cuban exiles and reorganizing the scattered revolutionary groups.

Antonio Maceo and Máximo Gómez, the Cuban military heroes of the Ten Years' War, were both furious at the way the Pact of Zanjón had been virtually ignored by the Spanish government. Both wanted to organize a new revolt against the Spanish. However, they could not do this without the financial support of Cuban émigrés in the United States. José Martí was only 29 years old, but he was already one of the leaders of New York's Cuban population. If Cuba was to be independent, Gómez and Maceo would need Martí's help and he would need their help.

In 1882, Martí wrote to the two generals to introduce himself. He told them that the revolution had not died and that he was eager to help them. He wanted them all to get together and prepare a plan of revolt with the help of New York's Cuban émigrés. Martí thought that the time was right in Cuba for yet another Cuban revolt. In response to Martí's letter, Maceo wrote: "My sword and my last breath are at the service of Cuba [but] I believe that for the new struggle we need unity of action, organization and money; none of these have been made available to me in my efforts to see my Patria free and fulfilled."[33]

Quarrel With Gómez and Maceo

In the summer of 1884, Gómez and Maceo came to New York to meet with Martí and other Cuban revolutionaries in exile. Gómez and Maceo were both military men. They did not want to discuss politics but only wanted money to support an invasion of the island. At first, neither general fully trusted Martí, who was younger than they were and did not have military credentials or battlefield experience. Martí also supported a civilian rather than military government and was known as a poet. Nevertheless, both generals were impressed with Martí's spirit. The three men decided they could work together.

Gómez appointed Maceo and Martí to visit Cuban communities in the United States to raise money for the coming struggle. However, in October 1884, Martí talked about some of his own plans for financing and conducting the invasion. In response, Gómez said, "Look, Martí: You limit yourself to what you're instructed to do; for the rest, General Maceo will do what he must."[34]

Martí already distrusted dictatorship from his experiences in Venezuela and Guatemala. His firsthand observations of the dictator Porfirio Díaz in Mexico had convinced him that a government controlled by the army was a dead-end path for Cuba. Martí had always believed, "The power enjoyed by republics should only be in the hands of civilians."[35] He worried that Gómez and Maceo considered the Cuban war of independence to be their own personal enterprise. Martí feared that the two generals intended to impose a military government in Cuba.

GENERAL MAXIMO GOMEZ.

General Máximo Gómez was one of the heroes of Cuba's Ten Years' War. He worked closely with José Martí to try to win Cuba's independence.

Martí wrote, "The patria belongs to no one, and if it does it will belong—and then only in spirit—to he who serves it with the greatest selflessness and intelligence."[36]

In October 1884, Martí felt that he had to separate from his powerful allies. To everyone's shock, Martí resigned from the movement. In Martí's famous "Letter to Máximo Gómez," he wrote that the two generals might bring Cuba a government of personal despotism more shameful and regrettable than the political despotism it now endures. . . . A nation is not founded, General, the way one commands a military camp. . . . What are we, General? Are we heroic, modest servants of an idea that fires our hearts, the loyal friends of a nation in distress? Or are we bold and fortune-favored caudillos [military dictators] who with whip in hand and spurs on our heels prepare to bring war to a nation in order to take possession of it for ourselves?[37]

Gómez was stunned. On the back of Martí's letter, he wrote an account of the incident that inspired it and added, "This man insults me recklessly."[38] The so-called Gómez-Maceo Insurrectional Plan lasted from August 1884 to September 1886 but, in spite of their efforts, they never were able to send an expedition to Cuba.

Martí was criticized in New York for withdrawing from the movement. Some Cuban revolutionaries claimed he was greedy and selfish, willing to halt the entire revolutionary struggle simply because he was jealous of Gómez and Maceo. This criticism, however, was nothing compared to Martí's own unhappiness. Cuba Libre seemed further away than ever. It appeared as if all his work in New York for the last five years had been for no purpose.

5

José Martí the Poet

José Martí was a practical man. He spent most of his life planning a military revolt in Cuba, yet he had little patience for people who thought poetry was unimportant. In an essay about the American poet Walt Whitman, Martí wrote, "Who is the ignoramus who maintains that people can dispense with poetry?" In fact, Martí believed poetry was "more necessary to a people than industry." This was because "industry gives men the means of subsistence, poetry gives them the desire and courage for living."[39]

Martí wrote all the time. Throughout his life, he jotted down anything that interested him on scraps of paper that he put in notebooks. Twenty of these notebooks remain. They are filled with quotations, current events, jokes, and anything that popped into his head at the time. Despite all the writing he did, Martí published only two small books of poetry during his entire lifetime—*Ismaelillo* and *Versos Sencillos*. This small output reflected Martí's concern with finding exactly the right words, tone, and content to make his poetry communicate his feelings. These two slim volumes have solidified Martí's reputation as one of the greatest and groundbreaking poets of the nineteenth century.

MARTÍ'S MODERNISMO

Martí's poetry opened the way for modernism (*modernismo*) in Spanish American literature. Modernismo was a movement that developed in Latin America in the 1890s. Modernist poetry often created strange and exotic landscapes filled with symbolic animals, colors, and flowers. Later American modernists rejected traditional Spanish rhyming patterns and instead used daring new rhythms and meters. They even wrote in free (nonrhyming) verse, often about very personal matters. Yet they tried to avoid the traditional Spanish overemphasis on sentiment or strong emotion and feeling.

The Nicaraguan poet Rubén Darío was the main figure in the modernismo movement. Darío always credited Martí as a founder of the movement. In 1888, Darío claimed that Martí "writes more brilliantly than any other in Spain or in America today."[40] Other major figures of the early modernist movement were the Colombian poet José Asunción Silva and the Cuban poet Julián del Casal.

Martí's modernist poetry had a huge impact on Latin American poetry. Nobel Prize–winning poet Gabriela Mistral, from Chile, later wrote: "All gratitude is in my love for Martí, gratitude for the writer who is the American Master most ostensible [apparent] in my work."[41] Martí did not completely break with the past. He sometimes used regular rhyming schemes. A poem like "La Niña de Guatemala" ("The Young Woman of Guatemala") is very sentimental, in the old Spanish tradition. Nonetheless, there was a real difference between Martí's symbolic and autobiographical poetry compared with the flowery work of other poets writing in Spanish in the 1800s.

VERSOS SENCILLOS (SIMPLE POETRY)

Versos Sencillos, Martí's most important book of poetry, was published in 1891. Most of these 46 short poems were written in the summer of 1890 after a winter of stress and sickness. His doctor advised him to take a much-needed rest in the Catskill Mountains of New York. The poems he wrote there sealed Martí's reputation as a master poet.

In the introduction to *Versos Sencillos*, Martí wrote, "My friends know how these poems come from my heart. . . . These poems are printed because . . . I love simplicity and believe in the need of putting one's feelings into plain and honest form."[42] Martí wrote most of *Versos Sencillos* in four-line stanzas. In each poem, he generally kept a constant rhyme scheme from stanza to stanza. The simplicity of the rhymes and the verses plays extremely well against the mysterious imagery of the content.

One of José Martí's favorite topics was the natural world. He had never felt completely at home among the crowds and bustle of New York City. A summer in the beautiful Catskills inspired him to contrast the inadequacy of human knowledge with the beauty and innocence of the fresh mountain air. An example of his fondness for the natural world can be found in Verso II:

> I know about Persia and Xenophon,
> Egypt and the Sudan,
> But I prefer to be caressed
> By fresh mountain air.
>
> I know the age-old history
> Of human grudges,
> But I prefer the bees that fly
> Among the bellflowers.[43]

Martí sometimes thought about the purpose of his own poetry. In Verso V, he used unusual metaphors to describe his poetry. The image of "daggers sprouting blossoms from the hilts" is very memorable. The last verse displays Martí's belief that his poetry was just another building block in creating a Cuba Libre:

> If you see a hill of foam,
> It is my poetry you see;
> My poems are mountains
> And feather fans.

> My poems are daggers
> Sprouting blossoms from the hilts;
> My poems are fountains
> Spraying jets of coral.

> My poems please the valiant;
> Sincere and brief; my poetry
> Is rugged as the steel they use
> To forge a sword.[44]

MARTÍ AND AUTOBIOGRAPHICAL POETRY

Most of José Martí's poems are autobiographical. Each poem captures a moment or fleeting sensation that affected him. In many poems, Martí opens his heart, mind, and soul to the reader's view. In Verso XXXV, he expressed the anger he felt toward his wife, Carmen Zayas Bazán, whom he felt had betrayed him by taking his son back to Cuba. Once again, a weapon is set against the role of poetry:

> What matters that your dagger
> Into my heart is plunged far?
> I have my verses which are
> More powerful than your dagger!

> What matters that this great pain
> Clouds the sky and drains the sea?

My verse, sweet solace to me,
Is born with the wings of pain.

Since 1880, Martí had been in love with Carmita Mantilla. In contrast to the anger he felt toward his wife, Martí clearly shows loving feelings for Carmita in this excerpt from Verso IV:

I will visit longingly
All the places where unseen
My lover and I have been
Playing with waves by the sea.

The two of us were alone
Except for the company
Of twin birds that we could see
Had to the dark cavern flown

Martí did not write for fame or fortune. He wrote poems because he felt he had to express his innermost feelings in plain words. Martí's poems sometimes reflected his inner confusion and unrest. In Verso XXIII, Martí considers his death and the ultimate judgment on his life:

I wish to leave the world
By its natural door;
In my tomb of green leaves
They are to carry me to die.

Do not put me in the dark
To die like a traitor;
I am good, and like a good thing
I will die with my face to the sun![45]

POETRY, POLITICS, AND SOCIAL JUSTICE

Unlike some modernists, Martí never let the art of his poetry completely replace his interest in political and economic change. Martí's desire to end slavery in Cuba and free the island from Spanish rule strengthened his writing. Many of his poems contain political or revolutionary rhetoric. In some poems, he condemned Spanish colonial rule in Cuba, attacked slavery, and identified with the oppressed people of the world. Martí's ability to mix poetry with the quest for social justice influenced many of Latin America's greatest twentieth-century poets such as Pablo Neruda, the 1971 Nobel Prize winner from Chile.

For example, in Verso XXX, Martí paints an appalling picture of the slave trade:

> The lightning the heaven scorches,
> And the clouds are bloodstained patches:
> The ship its hundreds disgorges
> Of captive blacks through the hatches.
>
> The fierce winds and brutal rains
> Beat against the dense plantation:
> In a file the slaves in chains
> Are led naked for inspection.[46]

In this excerpt from Verso XXVII, Martí describes the incident in 1869, when the Spanish opened fire on an unarmed crowd:

> The brutal enemy last night
> Our houses torched as we slept:
> The streets with his sword were swept,
> By the tropical moonlight.
>
> Few there were who had not bore
> The Spanish saber's wild fury:
> And at sunrise all could see
> The streets steeped in blood and gore.

In the 1960s, American folk singer and political activist Pete Seeger used some of José Martí's poems from *Versos Sencillos* and turned them into the popular song "Guántanamera."

GUÁNTANAMERA

Most English-speaking readers know of José Martí from the lyrics to the song "Guántanamera." The idea of using Martí's poems as the lyrics to a song originated with the Spanish composer Julián Orbón. Orbón lived in Havana from 1940 to 1963 and then moved to New York. One of Orbón's students gave his version of the song to North American musical legend Pete Seeger. In the early 1960s, Seeger popularized this version of "Guántanamera" with the lyrics by José Martí. In turn, the Sandpipers, a singing group, turned it into a huge top-10 hit on the American and British popular music charts. "Guántanamera" has been a well-known folk song since that time, using some of Martí's poems from *Versos Sencillos* around its famous chorus, Guántanamera, guajira

Guántanamera. (A *guajira Guántanamera* is either a girl or a song from the Cuban town of Guantánamo.)

> I am an honest man
> From where the palms grow;
> Before I die I want my soul
> To shed its poetry
>
> My poems are palest green
> And flaming scarlet;
> A wounded deer that searches for
> A refuge in the forest.
>
> With the poor of the earth
> I wish to share my fate
> The stream of the mountain
> Pleases me more than the sea.[47]

OTHER NOTABLE POETRY

Most of Martí's best poetry comes from the period when he lived in New York. Between 1878 and 1882, Martí wrote the poems included in *Versos Libres*. Although they were written about the same time as *Ismaelillo*, they were not published until 1913, long after his death.

In the introduction to *Versos Libres*, Martí wrote, "These are my poems. They are what they are. I have not borrowed them from anyone. As long as I was unable to lock up my visions whole, and in a form worthy of them, I let them fly."[48]

The poems are free in form. Martí's subject matter is also wide-ranging. Unlike *Versos Sencillos*, these poems have no consistent rhyming pattern. However, their meter is regular. Each line in Spanish contains roughly 11 syllables. These free verses are far more disordered and complex than Martí's "simple verses." This may be why he did not publish them in his lifetime.

Martí's most famous political poem is probably "*Dos Patrias*" ("Two Patrias"). It was also written in the 1880s but not published until 1913. The speaker is a woman who, like Martí, yearns for freedom to come to Cuba even though the island is in darkness. The setting sun symbolized the despair of the people, but while hope may seem gone, the sun will always rise tomorrow. The following excerpt is from the first stanza of "Dos Patrias":

JOSÉ MARTÍ AND THE NOVEL

José Martí loved poetry because he thought it revealed the deepest truths about human existence. He did not like novels because he did not think long fiction was serious enough. He complained that novels were too unreal, and grumbled about dialogues that had never been spoken between people who had never lived.

Martí did try to write one novel, entitled *Amistad Funesta* (*Fatal Friendship*; sometimes known as *Lucia Jerez*). It was published in installments in 1885 in a bimonthly New York magazine called *El Latino-Americano*. Martí wrote it as a favor for a friend and supposedly it only took him a week to write. Martí published it anonymously under the name Adelaida Ral, perhaps because one of the themes of the novel dealt with female homosexuality.

As a critic, however, Martí enjoyed novels and admired some novelists. Martí particularly liked writers who were concerned with politics. He thought very highly of Harriet Beecher Stowe, who wrote *Uncle Tom's Cabin*, an attack on slavery, in 1852. He also respected Helen Hunt Jackson, whose writings defended Native Americans. Martí translated her famous novel, *Ramona*, into Spanish in 1884. In several essays, Martí also praised the U.S. novelists Mark Twain (*Huckleberry Finn*), Nathaniel Hawthorne (*The Scarlet Letter*), and Louisa May Alcott (*Little Women*).

I have two countries: Cuba and the night.
Or are both one? No sooner does the sun
Withdraw its majesty, than Cuba,
With long veils and holding a carnation,
Appears as a sad and silent widow. [49]

THE CRITIC

Martí's influence on poetry went far beyond his own writings. In essay after essay, Martí introduced the works of North America's greatest poets to the Hispanic world. He wrote about famous nineteenth-century North American poets such as Henry Wadsworth Longfellow and John Greenleaf Whittier. Martí's work allowed Latin American writers to look to the United States for inspiration instead of just to Europe.

Martí's favorite poet in the United States was Walt Whitman, the author of "Leaves of Grass." Whitman is now considered the greatest North American poet, but he wasn't renowned at the time of his death in 1892. Martí always thought Whitman was brilliant. In 1887, Martí wrote about Whitman: "He must be studied because though he is not always in the best of taste, he is the most audacious, all-encompassing, and unencumbered poet of his time. . . ." He praised Whitman's language, "entirely different from that which poets before him have used."[50] Martí felt that he was doing the same thing in Spanish by introducing a fresh voice into the flowery language of traditional Spanish literature.

Martí particularly admired North American writer and poet Ralph Waldo Emerson, whom he called the "Philosopher of Democracy." Martí loved Emerson's descriptions of nature; he said that Emerson's poetry "pounds and surges like waters of the seas. . . . [O]ther poems of his are like trickles of precious stones, or shreds of cloud, or shards of lightning." Martí also respected Emerson, like Whitman, for his independent thought. Martí wrote, "Neither his mind nor his tongue nor his conscience was for hire."[51]

José Martí had great respect for American poet Walt Whitman, who used a fresh new style that made him stand out from earlier poets.

Perhaps most importantly, Martí identified with Emerson's idea that the poet was closer to the truth than the scientist or the philosopher. Although Martí spent his life in the real world, working for Cuban independence, he never lost the sense that poetry was a bridge into a world that was even more real.[52]

6

José Martí and the United States

José Martí used New York as a home base for the last 15 years of his life. He wrote hundreds of articles with detailed descriptions, compliments, and criticisms of the United States. Martí's writings are one of the best analyses of life in the United States in the late 1800s. Martí's perspective as an outside observer who knew the country well adds an interesting dimension to his letters.

Martí always viewed the United States from a Latin American perspective. This viewpoint was his natural style but it was also required because he was often writing for newspapers in South America and Central America. Martí used his "Letters from New York" to try to give the Latin American majority of the Western Hemisphere a better understanding of the United States. He also hoped to use his analysis of the United States to encourage his ideal of Latin American unity.

When Martí first arrived in the United States, his view was extremely positive. He had come to a land that he admired and

José Martí wrote one of his most famous pieces about Coney Island, the popular New York tourist attraction. Located in Brooklyn, Coney Island was the largest amusement park in the United States in the late 1800s and early 1900s.

respected. In July 1880, even before he moved permanently to New York, Martí wrote of his first "Impressions of America" for *The Hour*:

> I am, at last, in a country where every one looks like his own master. One can breathe freely, freedom being here the foundation, the shield, the essence of life. One can be proud of his species here. Every one works, every one reads. . . . I am deeply obliged to this country, where the friendless find always a friend and a kind hand is always found by those who look honestly for work.[53]

This type of praise filled Martí's early writings. He admired democracy and, at first, complimented the United States as a true popular democracy. The bustle of Gilded Age New York City astonished him. In his famous piece on Coney Island in 1881, Martí focused on what seemed to him to be the boundless energy of the North American people, even when they were relaxing. He wrote:

> But what coming and going! What torrents of money! What facilities for pleasure! What absolute absence of any outward

sadness or poverty! Everything in the open air . . . This spending, this uproar, these crowds, the activity of this amazing ant hill never slackens from June to October, from morning 'till night, without pause, without interruption, without variation.[54]

INDUSTRIALIZATION AND MATERIALISM

Martí admired the small farmers and shop owners of Cuba. He thought their lives would be happy and prosperous if only Cuba had an independent government that was elected by the people. However, Martí discovered that this way of life was disappearing in the United States. Large-scale industrialization meant that a few giant businesses known as corporations dominated the production of goods. These corporations were replacing the small farmers and independent businesspeople of the United States. In the future, people were more likely to work for a salary for an employer than to work for themselves. The divisions between rich and poor were growing larger. In many articles, Martí discussed the rise of corporations and the super rich. He complained that,

> Exclusive wealth is unfair. Let it belong to the many, not to the recent arrivals, the new hands without a purpose, but to the men who honestly and industriously deserve it. A nation having many small landowners is rich. A nation having a few wealthy men is not rich, only the one where each of its inhabitants shares a little of the common wealth. In political economy and in good government, distribution is the key to prosperity.[55]

Martí also realized that the industrialization of the United States would be a problem for Latin America. An industrializing country would need a source of raw materials. It would also need a place to sell all the extra goods that it produced. Martí feared that industrialization would lead the United States to try to dominate the Caribbean and South America.

Martí intensely disliked materialism—the desire for wealth and material possessions with little interest in ethical or spiritual matters. He thought that the United States in the Gilded Age had declined from its noble origins. It had replaced its tradition of freedom and dignity with a "religion" of selfish materialism. Martí noted bitterly that the most common traits found in North Americans were "widespread spiritual coarseness. . . . Everybody fighting for themselves. Achieving a fortune is the only objective desired."[56] He hoped that Cubans would never come to love money like the people of the United States did, because, "slavery would be better than this kind of liberty; ignorance would be better than this dangerous science."[57] Martí described North Americans as, "This splendid sick people, in one side wonderfully extended, in another side—that of intellectual pleasures—childish and poor."[58]

ATTACKS ON IMMIGRATION

In the late 1800s, millions of immigrants came to the United States to look for jobs in the industrializing society. Martí was not always sympathetic to these people. He felt that they were motivated by greed rather than the desire to experience the freedom that some were denied in their native countries. He complained that immigrants brought "their hatreds, their wounds, their moral ulcers"[59] to the United States.

In 1880, Martí wrote that "the common people, increased every day by a thirsty foreign population . . . [with an] anxious desire for money" must not be confused with "the true Americans [who] preserve national greatness, constitutional rights, old and honorable names, from the vulgar storm of immigration."[60]

Yet Martí could occasionally be supportive of immigrants and their customs. In "The Lynching of the Italians," Martí publicized an incident in 1891 about a mob that broke into a New Orleans jail and lynched 11 Italians. He wrote with horror about anti-immigrant feelings in the United States that could so easily break into violence.

DISILLUSIONMENT

The longer Martí lived in the United States, the less he liked what he saw. He began to write a great deal about the huge differences between the rich and the poor in New York City. Martí also noted the racism all around him. In "A Town Sets a Black Man on Fire," Martí wrote movingly on an incident in which, "Texans and Arkansans gathered, both women and men, and set fire to a Negro drenched in gasoline who was tied to a pine tree."[61] Martí was particularly sensitive to the plight of Native Americans in the United States. He criticized the leaders of the United States who "believe in the inferiority of the black race, whom they enslaved yesterday and denigrate today, and of the Indians, whom they are exterminating."[62]

Martí also soured on the United States as a model of democracy. Throughout the 1880s, he wrote about corruption in the election process and how big corporations dominated the government. He grumbled that big business did not allow honest people to serve the country in elected office. In 1889, Martí wrote, "What is apparent is that the nature of the North American government is gradually changing. . . . [T]he republic is becoming plutocratic [run by the rich] and imperialistic."[63]

Martí warned his readers repeatedly that North American control of the Caribbean region would be a disaster for Cuba. He condemned the United States for taking over Samoa in 1889 and Hawaii in 1890. Martí did not attack the United States alone. He also criticized British colonialism in Egypt, India, and Ireland, and French colonialism in Tunisia and Vietnam. In *La Edad de Oro*, he praised the resistance of the Vietnamese to attacks by Chinese, Siamese (now Thailand), and French invaders. Martí always stressed the need to fight against outside intruders.

By 1889, Martí no longer thought the United States was an inspiration for a liberated Cuba. He stated that Cubans "admire this nation [the United States], the greatest ever built by liberty, but they dislike the evil conditions that, like worms in the heart, have begun in this mighty republic their work of destruction."[64] Martí began using the United States as a model of what to avoid in the future Cuban republic. He wrote:

> In the sins [the United States] commits, its errors, where it falls short—it is necessary to study this people, in order that we will not make the same mistakes. . . . It is a great nation, the only one where a man can truly achieve greatness. However, both through a constant pride in its prosperity and the fact that in order to maintain its vast appetite it is always overextended, this people falls into a moral vacuum, its better senses poisoned, adoring—wrongly—success above all.[65]

Martí did not hate the United States, but he did not love the country, either. He clearly saw two sides to the United States—one that he admired and the other that he disliked. By the time Martí wrote "The Truth about the United States" in 1894 for a Latin American audience, the Truth Martí described was mostly negative.

NUESTRA AMÉRICA (OUR AMERICA)

Martí's most widely read essay today is *"Nuestra América"* ("Our America"), which was published in newspapers in New York and Mexico City in January 1891. In this essay, Martí stated that there was a basic difference between those American societies produced by the cultures of Catholic Spain and Portugal and those produced by Protestant Great Britain.

For Martí, this fact meant that Latin Americans should not automatically copy foreign political systems that came from a completely different experience in the United States. From living in Mexico, Guatemala, and Venezuela, Martí knew that Latin Americans had their own unique needs and desires. He wrote, "To govern well, one must attend closely to the reality of the place that is governed. . . . The government must be born from the country. . . . The form of the government must be in harmony with the country's natural constitution."[66]

Martí warned that the United States was poised to expand into Latin America. In "Nuestra América," Martí called the United States "the giant with the seven-league boots who can crush" Latin America underfoot. Martí believed that as long as the United States looked down on Spanish America as inferior, there was no point in forming any economic or political union with the giant to the north. He warned that, "Our America may face another danger . . . the hour is near when she will be approached by an enterprising and forceful nation [the United States] that will demand intimate relations with her, though it does not know her and disdains her." The only possible response that could succeed depended on the cooperation between the nations of "nuestra América."[67]

THE DIPLOMAT

Martí's fame as a writer led to a brief career in diplomacy. Even though he was a Cuban exile living in the United States, Martí was appointed vice-consul for Uruguay in New York in 1884 and 1887, and for Argentina and Paraguay in 1890. He was also Uruguay's delegate to the First International Conference of American States (1889–1890) and to the International Monetary Conference (1891). Martí played an especially important role at these two conferences.

The Conference of American States was the idea of U.S. Secretary of State James Blaine. Blaine was the leading figure in the Republican Party in the 1870s and 1880s. He supported U.S. business interests and believed that the government should work hard to expand U.S. trading opportunities, especially in Latin America. Blaine wanted Latin American countries to open their borders to trade and investment from the United States. He also supported U.S. foreign expansion. In 1891, Blaine wrote to President Benjamin Harrison: "I think there are only three places that are of value and not already taken, that are not continental. . . . One is Hawaii and the others are Cuba and Puerto Rico."

Martí intensely disliked Blaine and his schemes. Martí believed that all the talk in Washington, D.C., about the cooperation of nations in the Western Hemisphere was simply a disguised attempt by the United States to take over Latin America. In one speech, Martí urged the delegates to declare their "second independence," this time from the United States.

BEING HISPANIC

JOSÉ MARTÍ'S LOVE OF LATIN AMERICA

José Martí's whole worldview revolved around being Hispanic. His essay "Our America" summed up a lifetime's thought on the unity of Latin American nations and their basic differences with the United States.

Martí wanted all Latin American nations to establish close political, commercial, and cultural ties. He disliked the idea that the people of "our America" regarded themselves mainly as Argentineans, Mexicans, or whatever their specific nationality before Latin Americans. He loved Latin America but complained that petty interests prevented the so-called sister-republics from acting cooperatively. For Martí, Latin American revolutionaries such as Simón Bolívar, José de San Martín, and Miguel Hidalgo y Costilla were role models and heroes for the Cuban independence movement even though they had never fought in Cuba.

In "Our America," Martí wrote, "We must advance shoulder-to-shoulder, one solid mass like the silver lodes in the depths of the Andes."* In order to do this, Latin Americans had to accept their multiracial identity. It was in "Our America" where Martí famously said, "There is no racial hatred, because there are no races. . . . The soul, equal and eternal, emanates from bodies that are diverse in form and color."

Martí was a realist. He had lived in three Latin American nations and understood their problems and their strengths. Throughout his life, he was proud to be both Cuban and Hispanic. His philosophy could be summed up in his quotation, "The wine I like is from the banana; and if it is sour I do not care, because it is our wine!"**

* José Martí. *The America of José Martí: Selected Writings*, Juan de Onís, trans (New York: Noonday Press, 1953), 139.

** Christopher Abel and Nissa Torrents, eds. *José Martí: Revolutionary Democrat* (Durham, N.C.: Duke University Press, 1986), 116.

U.S. Secretary of State James Blaine encouraged Latin American countries to open their borders to U.S. trade and investment. In 1889, he chaired the First International Conference of American States, in which José Martí took part.

The same themes arose the next year at the Inter-American Monetary Conference. The United States, allied with silver-producing nations such as Mexico and Peru, tried to convince other nations to accept silver on equal terms to gold as a currency. As the delegate from Uruguay, Martí argued that the new standard might weaken Latin American currencies and strengthen the United States. Martí's influence was crucial and the proposal did not pass.

After the Monetary Conference, Martí explained his fears of the United States. He wrote, "Whoever says economic union says political union. The nation that buys, commands. The nation that sells, serves. Commerce must be balanced to assure freedom. The nation eager to die sells to a single nation, and the one eager to save itself sells to more than one."[68]

Martí's place in all these negotiations led to some complaints from diplomats. They argued that it was not proper for a Cuban revolutionary in exile to represent another country at an international conference. Martí resigned from his diplomatic positions. From 1891 on, he devoted himself exclusively to the struggle for Cuban independence.

THE VINDICATION OF CUBA

The United States had thought about taking over Cuba ever since Thomas Jefferson's presidency in the early 1800s. It was a valuable supplier of sugar and its position in the Caribbean made it important to relations with Mexico and Central America. Before the U.S. Civil War, Southerners worked hard, though unsuccessfully, to either buy or steal Cuba from Spain and make it a slave state. In the 1880s, there was also talk of building a canal across Panama or Nicaragua to connect the Atlantic and Pacific oceans. If this canal were built, Cuba's position in the Caribbean would become even more important.

The Ten Years' War, which ended in 1878, had bankrupted many Cuban plantation owners. After the war, many North American companies purchased sugar plantations and refineries in Cuba. The power and influence of the United States increased in Cuba every year. Once again, there was talk in the United States of taking or buying Cuba from Spain.

Not everyone in the United States wanted to annex Cuba, however. Some people opposed North American imperialism while others were outright racists. In 1889, the newspaper the *Philadelphia Manufacturer* published an editorial entitled, "Do We Want Cuba?" The editor argued that the Cuban population—made up of poor criollos, corrupt Spaniards, and slaves—was helpless, idle, and immoral. According to the newspaper, Cubans were "unfitted by nature and experience for discharging the obligations of citizenship in a great and free republic." It would be silly to allow Cubans to vote because "they have not the slightest capacity."[69]

Martí was outraged at the ignorance and prejudice. He was also stunned that North Americans considered Cuba, his patria, just another piece of merchandise to be acquired. In response, he wrote a reply entitled "Vindication of Cuba," published on March 25, 1889, in the *New York Evening Post*. In this long and powerful essay, Martí argued that Cuban culture was the product of a civilized, knowledgeable, and politically aware society. He cited the hard work and intelligence of the Cuban community in exile: "Cubans are found everywhere, working as farmers, surveyors, engineers, mechanics, teachers, journalists."

The "Vindication of Cuba" also noted the bravery of the Cuban population in rebelling against the corrupt Spanish colonial system. He declared that Cubans were not a "country of petty talkers, incapable of action, hostile to hard work. . . . We have suffered impatiently under tyranny; we have fought like men, sometimes like giants, to be freemen." In fact, Martí remarked that the U.S. government had remained neutral in the Ten Years' War. This cowardice on the part of the United States had allowed Spanish colonial rule and tyranny to continue in Cuba.

Martí went so far as to say that Cubans did not want to become a part of a country as self-centered as the United States. He wrote that "no self-respecting Cuban would like to see his country annexed to a nation where the leaders of opinion share towards him the prejudices excusable only to vulgar jingoism or rampant ignorance."[70]

Because Martí lived in the United States for so long, he sensed that the United States was about to expand into the Caribbean and Latin America. He feared that this economic and political domination would occur before Cuba won its independence. Martí redoubled his efforts to begin a Cuban revolution as soon as possible.

7

The Cuban Revolutionary Party

Between 1892 and 1895, José Martí devoted himself completely to the cause of Cuban independence. He gave speeches, wrote pamphlets, and had articles published in newspapers to raise political and financial support. He organized Cuban exiles into the Cuban Revolutionary Party and published a newspaper devoted to Cuban freedom. In all these efforts, Martí received help from the Cuban community in exile, especially those Cubans living in New York and Florida.

During the Ten Years' War, many Havana cigar manufacturers had moved to Key West, Florida, to avoid the conflict. This was convenient because the southern tip of Florida was less than 100 miles from Cuba. Making cigars in Florida also made it easier to sell cigars in the United States. Cigar manufacturers found themselves limited in Key West, however, because it was a small island with few skilled laborers.

When the railroad arrived in Tampa, Florida, in 1884, that city became attractive to Cuban business owners. Vicente Martínez

Ybor City in Tampa, Florida, was home to many Cuban immigrants, as well as a political newspaper that continued to inspire the Cuban revolution. The section of Tampa was also known for its cigar factories.

Ybor, a cigar-maker in Key West, bought 40 acres of land near downtown Tampa in 1885 and opened a cigar-making factory. Soon, the area known as Ybor City, and later developments in nearby West Tampa, Palmetto Beach, and Port Tampa, became centers of a thriving Spanish-language culture. In the 1890s, several thousand Italian immigrants also moved to Ybor City. Tampa became a multiethnic manufacturing port complete with labor organizations and ethnic clubs. Ybor City and Key West both earned reputations as homes to activist workers and radical politics. In Key West, the newspaper *El Yara*, which first appeared in 1876, helped keep the ideals of the Cuban war of independence alive.

Cuban immigrants in Florida reflected all the social classes and skin colors of Cuban urban society. Middle-class professionals, cigar workers, and business owners all mixed together. Many cigar manufacturers, such as Ybor, supported Cuban independence. Ybor even allowed workers to collect funds for a Cuban revolution in his facilities. The Cuban revolutionaries in Florida were extremely active and powerful. Spanish General Martínez Campos complained that Tampa was "the very heart of the American conspiracy" to liberate Cuba.[71]

In the Tampa area, black and white Cubans lived side by side. This type of tolerance was amazing, especially for a Southern state in the 1890s. "White and Negro Cubans lived in harmony," wrote José Rivero Muñiz, a contemporary observer, "all being admitted without exception to the various revolutionary clubs, none ever protested." Although Muñiz overstated the degree of friendship, there was some truth in his claim that, "the relations between Cuban whites and Negroes were most cordial and there was no racial discrimination. . . . They were mutually respectful."[72]

José Martí had a high opinion of the Cuban exile communities in Tampa and Key West. In fact, Martí would visit Tampa more than 20 times during his life. He wrote admiringly that in Cuban Florida, "the physician forgets the luxuries of Paris in the little home he has purchased for his wife with the sweat of his brow. . . . [T]he sullen guerrilla fighter, kind and strong-armed, takes his children to school on his way to work by the same arm that once led a stallion through the bush." The area seemed to resemble what Cuba might look like if it ever became independent.[73]

JOSÉ MARTÍ AND RACE RELATIONS

One of the things that José Martí most admired about Cuban Florida was its relative racial tolerance. Martí felt that good race relations were essential for starting a successful revolution in Cuba. He constantly tried to encourage Cuban nationalism and play down racial differences. Martí called for unity and cooperation by various social groups, classes, and races to achieve independence. Martí needed to take this position because of the makeup of Cuba's population.

Several different groups of native peoples, such as the Arawak and the Ciboney, inhabited Cuba when Christopher Columbus arrived in 1492 to claim the island for Spain. The native population was quickly destroyed by disease and mistreatment under Spanish rule. The Spanish replaced these natives with African slaves. At the same time, the European population grew from immigration, mainly from Spain, but also from other Latin American countries. As Cuban sugar production increased, so did the slave trade, which reached its peak in 1817. In 1867, Cuba had a total population of 1.37 million people. Of these, 765,000 (56 percent) were considered "white" and 605,000 (44 percent) were "black." Cuba's independence movement was generally much stronger in the eastern provinces, where the people tended to be poor and darker-skinned.

The Spanish and other enemies of revolution argued that an independent Cuba would lead to a slave uprising or a race war. The Spanish were able to divide the black and criollo Cuban revolutionaries by claiming that black leaders, such as Antonio Maceo, were really trying to create a "Negro Republic." During the Ten Years' War, this type of accusation forced Maceo out of his high position in the army. Martí wrote Maceo in 1882 that "in my view the solution to the Cuban problem is not political but a social one, and this can be accomplished only by that mutual love and forgiveness on the part of both races."[74]

Spain had abolished slavery in Cuba in 1886, but the Spanish continued to claim that any revolution would lead to a race war. Martí tried to counter this argument in an essay entitled "*Mi Raza*" ("My Race"), which was published in April 1893. In this essay, Martí claimed that the Ten Years' War not only led to the abolition of slavery but also eliminated all differences between blacks and whites. He wrote:

> In Cuba there is no fear whatever of racial conflict. . . . A Cuban is more than a mulatto, black, or white. Dying for Cuba on the battlefield, the souls of both negroes and white men have risen together. In the daily life of defense, loyalty, brotherhood . . . there has always been a Negro standing beside every white man. . . . There will never be a racial war in Cuba.[75]

As it turned out, more than half of the integrated Cuban revolutionary army in 1895 was of Afro-Cuban heritage.

Martí downplayed the issue of race, because he needed to unite the socially divided Cuban exiles behind Cuba Libre. He wrote,

> No man has any special rights because he belongs to one race or another: say "man" and all rights have been stated. The black man, as a black man, is not inferior or superior to any other man. . . . Anything that divides men from each other, that separates them, singles them out, or hems them in, is a sin against humanity.[76]

This was an astonishing position to take in the United States, especially in the 1890s. At that time, the U.S. government was encouraging racial segregation and refusing to fight racial violence, such as the lynching of African Americans.

ESTABLISHMENT OF LA LIGA

Martí knew that a successful revolution in Cuba needed black support. He therefore tried to win the backing of some Afro-Cubans in Florida, such as Cornelio Brito and Ruperto and Paulina Pedroso. The Pedrosos were Cuban-born descendants of slaves. They became some of Martí's fiercest supporters after meeting him in Key West. They later moved to Ybor City to work in a cigar factory and opened a boardinghouse and tavern there. When Martí visited Tampa, he stayed at the Pedroso boardinghouse. Ruperto slept in the hallway outside Martí's door to prevent any assassination attempts.[77]

Martí also worked with Rafael Serra, an Afro-Cuban exile, to form *La Liga* (The League). This was an educational center devoted to the advancement of black Cubans in the United States. For Martí, the creation of La Liga was a crucial part of starting a revolution in Cuba. Martí worked to find teachers, locate meeting rooms, and increase the number of members. He even taught a class every Thursday night. In a letter to Rafael Serra, Martí explained his reasons for working so hard on the La Liga project. He wrote, "Let us never forget that the greater the suffering, the greater the right to justice, and that the prejudices of men and social inequalities cannot prevail over the equality which nature has created."[78]

FOUNDING OF CUBAN REVOLUTIONARY PARTY

Martí made his first trip to Florida in November 1891. He was visiting Ybor City and Tampa at the request of José Dolores Poyo, Fernando Figueredo, and other leading Cubans in Florida. Martí hoped that he could reach out to the Florida workers' communities and unite them with the older New York Cuban groups. To do this, Martí would have to convince Florida's Cubans to contribute political support and money to his cause.

Much depended on the success of his mission, both for Cuba and for Martí personally. His diplomatic career had come to an end and his connections to the Gómez-Maceo military wing of the revolution were strained. Martí desperately needed the assistance of the Cuban tobacco workers of Ybor City, West Tampa, and Key West. If they would not support his vision of Cuban independence, Martí might spend the rest of his life just writing poetry and articles for newspapers in New York.

On November 26, 1891, Martí delivered a famous speech at the Cuban Lyceum in Tampa. The title of the speech, "Everyone Together and for the Well-Being of All," represented Martí's image of an independent Cuba. In this speech, Martí painted a shimmering picture of the future Cuba as a land of racial harmony and justice for all Cubans. Martí gave another speech the next day, which happened to be the twentieth anniversary of the shooting of the eight medical students by the Havana Volunteers in 1871. In it, Martí urged his Cuban audience to rise to the heroism and sacrifice needed to win the independence of Cuba. If they did, he said, Cubans would "sing today an anthem to life before their well remembered graves."[79]

Both of Martí's speeches were successful beyond his wildest dreams. Martí became very influential among the Cuban communities in Florida. He met with the members of the Cuban Patriotic League of Tampa. With a little help, Martí wrote two documents now known as the "Tampa Resolutions" and the "Bases of the Cuban Revolutionary Party." Martí placed great hopes in this Cuban Revolutionary Party (abbreviated PRC for its Spanish name, the *Partido Revolucionario Cubano*). He hoped that the PRC could unite all local Cuban patriotic organizations and social and revolutionary clubs. As an organization, the PRC would raise money and encourage people in Cuba to rebel against the Spanish. In January 1892, Martí drafted the general organizing principles of the PRC at a political rally in Ybor City.

Martí then returned to New York City. On March 14, 1892, he published the first issue of a new Spanish-language paper called *La Patria*. This newspaper, which Martí edited, became the official voice of the PRC. The PRC's existence, with Martí at its head, was officially announced in April 1892. The group's first goal was "to achieve with the united efforts of all men of good-will the complete independence of the island of Cuba, and to encourage and assist with the independence of Puerto Rico."[80]

THE FERNANDINA PLAN

Martí traveled widely through the United States, the Caribbean, and Central America trying to raise money for the PRC. He organized Cuban patriotic clubs in New York and along the East Coast. He inspired crowds with his passionate speeches and appointed local representatives to the party. He tried to build an underground network in Cuba that would recognize the authority of the PRC and take orders from the organization. Martí sent agents into Cuba to make contact with the rebel groups on the island.

In April 1894, Máximo Gómez and Martí met in New York and came up with a daring plan. They arranged an invasion of Cuba by a small group of trained soldiers led by the exiled leaders of the Ten Years' War. The two men hoped that a general uprising by the underground revolutionary forces in Cuba would break out at the same time.

The invasion plan had three parts. Maceo would launch an invasion from Costa Rica to land in Oriente province. Martí and his men would sail to the Dominican Republic, take Gómez aboard, and land him with 200 men in southern Cuba. A third expedition would leave directly from Florida and invade the Camaguey province in the central part of the island.

In order to do this, Martí assembled three ships he had bought with PRC funds. The vessels docked at Fernandina Beach, located on Amelia Island in northeast Florida. Amelia Island is the most southern of the Sea Islands that parallel the Carolina and Georgia coasts. At Fernandina, one of the oldest cities in Florida, the rebels loaded the boats with weapons and supplies. Because of this key location, the plan for a Cuban revolt was sometimes called the Fernandina Filibuster. A filibuster

JOSÉ MARTÍ'S RELATIONSHIP WITH MÁXIMO GÓMEZ AND ANTONIO MACEO

An independent Cuba would almost certainly have to earn its independence on the battlefield. To do this, Martí's PRC had to have the help of the military veterans of the Ten Years' War. Most of the officers of the rebel army were in exile in various countries in Latin America. Many had remained informed about the situation in Cuba and plotted against the Spanish government.

Máximo Gómez and Antonio Maceo were the two great military heroes of the Ten Years' War. If Martí had their support, then his cause had a chance. Unfortunately, Martí had quarreled with both of them in 1884. Martí knew it was now time to forget their past arguments. Martí and Gómez exchanged friendly letters and Martí visited him in the Dominican Republic. They met at Gómez's ranch at Montecristi near the capital city of Santo Domingo. The two men came to an agreement that the PRC, headed by Martí, would prepare for a war of independence against Spain and that Gómez would conduct the war as commander in chief of the army.

Martí next tried to make peace with Antonio Maceo. In 1891, Maceo had moved to Costa Rica to start an agricultural colony of Cuban exiles on the Pacific Coast. In 1892, Maceo visited the United States and contacted Martí. Later, Martí visited Maceo in Costa Rica twice to plan a revolt against Spain. By 1894, Martí and Maceo were friendly enough for Maceo to defend Martí against criticisms in a Cuban Key West newspaper.

Martí, Gómez, and Maceo were all brilliant, competent, strong-willed, brave, and totally committed to Cuban independence. They respected each other's abilities but did not always agree on the best strategy or tactics to use. However, this did not keep them from working together for the cause of Cuba Libre. Cubans consider all three men to be among their greatest heroes.

José Martí, Máximo Gómez, and Antonio Maceo were some of the most famous leaders of the struggle for Cuban independence. Martí, Gómez, and Maceo are pictured on this poster with Salvador Cisneros, president of the cabinet of the Cuban Republic, and Calixto García, commander of the Cuban Army during the Spanish-American War.

(from the Spanish *filibustero*, meaning "adventurer" or "pirate") was a private soldier, or expedition, that invaded another country.

FAILURE AND SUCCESS

The Fernandina Plan had a peculiar outcome. A member of the PRC accidentally revealed the plan to one of the captains of the ships. Soon the story spread along the Florida coast. The Spanish government heard the rumors and complained to the U.S. government. Filibustering was illegal and the U.S. government could not allow an invasion of another country by private citizens living in Florida. On January 10, 1895, the U.S. government confiscated the three vessels loaded with weapons at Fernandina Beach. Martí managed to escape back to New York but most of the men on board were arrested.

FILIBUSTERING

Before the Civil War, many white Southerners looked at Cuba as a slaveholding area that might be added to the United States. In 1848, President James Polk offered to buy Cuba from Spain for $100 million. In response, the Spanish minister declared, "Sooner than see the island transferred to any power, they would prefer seeing it sunk in the ocean."* If Spain would not give up Cuba peacefully, some private citizens would take the matter into their own hands. Although filibustering was illegal, many white Southerners supported these adventurers as a way to extend slave territory.

One of the most famous filibusters was the Venezuelan-born Narciso López. López tried three times to invade Cuba. In his second attempt in 1850, his three ships landed in Cuba and seized Cardenas, a small port eight miles east of Havana. The invaders had no popular support and most of the survivors fled back to Key West. In his third attempt, he led 400 armed men out of New Orleans on the steamer *Pampero*. A few of the rebels were Cuban exiles but most were young Southerners looking for adventure. After some early success, most of the men ended up dying of hunger or fatigue. Others, including López himself, were captured by the Spanish and brought to Havana for trial. After

To everyone's surprise, the failure of the Fernandina Plan did not crush the PRC. The idea that Martí had managed, against all odds, to organize such an ambitious scheme actually inspired the revolutionary movement. Cuban exile communities in New York and Florida rallied to support Martí. Even though the Fernandina Plan was a failure, the attempt convinced people that Martí was not just a mad poet but someone who was serious about organizing and fighting a Cuban revolt against the Spanish.

Martí wanted to take advantage of this wave of support. He pressed for a revolt to begin in Cuba as soon as possible. On January 29, 1895, less than three weeks after the failure of the

---

admitting to the charge of being hostile invaders, they were publicly executed.

Spain resented filibusters who left from U.S. territory. In retaliation, the Spanish sometimes harassed North American shipping. The most serious incident involved the *Black Warrior*, a merchant steamer that traveled from New York to Mobile, Alabama, usually stopping at Havana along the way. In 1854, Spanish authorities seized the ship and imposed a $6,000 fine for the violation of customs regulations. In at least 30 previous trips to Havana by the *Black Warrior*, Spanish authorities had ignored these regulations. The incident nearly caused a war between the United States and Spain until the Spanish government released the ship and paid $53,000 in damages.

Filibustering from the United States to Cuba peaked between 1848 and 1856 and declined after the U.S. Civil War. Some Cubans viewed these filibusters as heroes who dared to fight against the Spanish. Others saw them as conquerors who simply wanted to extend slavery.

  * Available online at *http://xroads.virginia.edu/~hyper/HNS/ Ostend/ostend.html*

Fernandina Plan, Martí, Gómez, and another member of the PRC issued an order for a general revolt in Cuba. The order called for a massive uprising "within the second fortnight [two weeks] of February, not before."[81] The order, addressed to Juan Gualberto Gómez, Martí's deputy within Cuba, was fittingly smuggled to the island inside a cigar that had been rolled in Florida.

Sure enough, fighting began at several locations on February 24, 1895. "The news of the breakout of the revolution in Cuba," announced the *Tampa Tribune*, "has kindled the sacred flames of patriotism of every Cuban altar in the city." Huge crowds gathered in front of cigar factories to hear news of the revolution while inside, workers listened to readers' accounts of the battles.[82] One by one, the Cuban leaders in exile slipped back to the island. In April 1895, José Martí returned to Cuba for the first time in nearly 16 years.

8

The Revolt Against Spain

After calling for an armed revolution in Cuba, José Martí left the United States and traveled to the Dominican Republic to join Máximo Gómez. He arrived at Montecristi on February 7, 1895, and waited for news that the uprising had begun. When this news arrived, Martí and Gómez would reenter Cuba.

However, problems arose when Antonio Maceo, living in Costa Rica, hesitated to join the invasion. On February 22, Maceo wrote to Martí complaining that the PRC had not given him enough money or weapons. Both Maceo and Gómez had doubts that Martí was the right person to organize the revolt. Maceo eventually agreed to participate, but he still questioned Martí's abilities.

From the Dominican Republic, Central America, and the United States, Cuban exile groups assembled to invade Cuba. On February 24, 1895, in the village of Baire, some Cuban exile forces united with the revolutionaries. They issued the *grito* or "cry" to begin the second war for Cuban independence.

The uprising against Spain that began in 1895 won the support of many people in Cuba. Some of the rebels are pictured here in a photograph taken in 1896.

However, spies had discovered that the uprising was going to occur. The Spanish government immediately arrested all the revolutionary leaders in Havana and put down the revolt in the western provinces. Once again, as had happened in the Ten Years' War, most of the fighting would take place in the east, especially in Oriente province.

CUBAN SUGAR AND U.S. FOREIGN RELATIONS

Now that the Cubans were again in revolt against Spain, everyone looked to see whether the U.S. government would side with either Spain or the Cuban rebels, or if it would remain neutral. The economy of Cuba depended on good economic relations with the United States, not Spain. By 1884, the United States received about 85 percent of everything produced in Cuba and 94 percent of the colony's sugar and molasses. Since 1865, North Americans had invested heavily in Cuban sugar mills, tobacco plantations, and mines. By the 1890s, they held nearly $50 million worth of property on the island.

President Benjamin Harrison's administration (1888–1892) had worked hard to boost trade with Cuba and kept the tariff (a tax on imports) on sugar low. From 1891 to 1893, U.S. trade with Cuba jumped considerably. Unfortunately, a huge economic depression, known as the Panic of 1893, swept the United States. In 1894, the U.S. Congress increased the tariff on Cuban goods to 40 percent and trade between the two nations collapsed.

The disintegration of Cuba's economy was a major reason for the popularity of the revolt against Spain in 1895. Unemployed Cubans with little hope for the future could see no further point in being a colony of Spain. Many joined the rebels, who again launched a guerrilla war against the Spanish and adopted a policy of deliberately burning sugar plantations. They hoped to damage what remained of the island's economy so much that the Spanish would want to leave.

Most North Americans who had investments in Cuba wanted the United States to somehow stop the war. They did not care who ruled Cuba as long as the revolution ended, the sugar fields stopped burning, and profits continued to be made. However, other business interests in the United States opposed an expanded role for the United States in Cuba. They feared that a war with Spain would upset the U.S. economy, which was only just starting to recover from the Panic of 1893. As a result, the U.S. government took a neutral position in 1895, watching the situation carefully but not getting involved. Meanwhile, Cubans in New York and Florida raised money, bought weapons, and launched a propaganda war. The Spanish government claimed that without this help from Cubans in the United States, the revolt would collapse.

MANIFESTO OF MONTECRISTI

Martí and Máximo Gómez were still in the Dominican Republic when the revolution broke out in eastern Cuba. On March 25, 1895, the two men signed the Manifesto of Montecristi, a document named after the small town where it was written. The manifesto, written mainly by Martí, was a long, detailed, and passionate document that described all the reasons that Cuba wanted and deserved independence from Spain. The Manifesto of Montecristi, like the U.S. Declaration of Independence, tried to justify the violence that was sure to follow when the revolt took place.

In the manifesto, Martí painted a dreamlike picture of Cuba after independence. It would no longer be dependent on sugar and its economy would not be dominated by the United States. Racial discrimination would end. Whites would appreciate, not fear, the Afro-Cuban population. Cuba would be a democratic republic, free from foreign influences or military control. Martí promised that, "this war will not be a cradle of tyranny or of disorder, which is alien to the proven moderation of the Cuban spirit. . . . We have no doubts about Cuba or its ability to obtain and govern its independence."[83]

Martí proudly noted that the revolution was not a minor event in world history. Instead, Cuba's strategic position in the Caribbean meant that the island would play a crucial role in world politics as the pivot between North and South America. He wrote, "The war of Cuban independence, located at the core of the Greater Antilles archipelago, which in a few years will be the crossroads of the commerce of two continents, is an event of the greatest human importance."[84] In a letter written the same day as the Manifesto of Montecristi, Martí wrote that the independence of Cuba would "preserve the independence and honor of our America . . . and will perhaps accelerate and stabilize the equilibrium of the world."[85]

ACTIONS, NOT LETTERS

Once the revolution broke out, many of Martí's friends thought he should return to New York. He was a small, middle-aged man who had never been a soldier. His personality and his pen were crucial to raising money in the United States for the revolt in Cuba. He was the glue that held the many different factions of the PRC together. However, Martí refused to return to the United States. A lifetime of working, planning, and hoping had gone into this attempt for Cuba's freedom. Martí wrote to a friend: "I promoted the war; with it my responsibility begins, not ends."[86]

Martí was always stung by accusations that he was not personally brave. In 1892, Enrique Collazo accused Martí of cowardice in an open letter to Martí that appeared in a Cuban newspaper. Collazo wrote, "If the hour of sacrifice comes again, we may not be able to shake your [Martí's] hand in the Cuban manigua—undoubtedly not, because you will still be giving the Cuban emigrants lessons in patriotism under the shadow of the American flag."[87] This type of attack really bothered Martí. He wrote that he would die of shame if he had asked others to give their lives for the Cuban war of independence while he was in New York. On March 25, 1895, Martí wrote to his mother, "[W]hy was I born from you with a life that loves sacrifice? . . . The duty of a man lies where he is most useful."[88]

Martí would not be particularly useful in Cuba unless he died there. As a martyr, he would be a powerful symbol for the Cuban cause. Since he had been a child, Martí had been fascinated by the concept of dying for one's patria. Now, he wrote what he called his last instructions to Federico Henriquez, a friend of his from the Dominican Republic. He also wrote to a friend named Gonzalo de Uesada, detailing what he wanted done with all his papers and manuscripts if he died. Martí wrote, "These books have been my vice and my luxury. . . . I never had the ones I wanted, nor did I think I had the right to buy any that were not needed for the task."[89] Martí had a strong feeling that he was going to die in Cuba.

In 1888, Martí had written, "One should not write with letters, but with actions."[90] Now he would have a chance to live out that belief. Just before he left Montecristi to return to Cuba, Martí wrote a farewell poem. It would be his last:

Goodbye. The boat leaves
Next week.
Now you have a friend
Who's leaving.

And of me I must say
That following serenely,
Without fear of the lightning and thunder
I am working out the future.[91]

RETURN TO CUBA

On April 1, Martí, Gómez, three Cubans, and one Dominican left Montecristi for Cuba. This was a smaller number than the group of 200 men that Martí and Gómez had planned to command, but they were committed to returning to Cuba now. The captain arranged to take them to the island of Great Inagua, a British colony and one of the islands of the Bahamas, and from there they would go to Cuba. When they reached Great Inagua, the captain instead alerted the authorities. The British searched the boat but found no weapons. The men were allowed to go free but they appeared to be stranded.

On Great Inagua, Martí became friends with Heinrich Lowe, captain of the steamship *Nordstrand*, which was bound for Haiti. Martí bribed the captain to bring Martí's group aboard and drop them off in a small boat near the coast of Cuba. On April 10, the *Nordstrand* passed the shore of Cuba at Cape Maisi. The six men put their weapons and supplies in a small rowboat. The weather was bad and the boat overloaded. Martí wrote in his diary:

The boat is lowered. Hard rain as we push off. Wrong direction. Opinions on boat varied and turbulent. More squalls. Lose rudder. We set course. I take the forward oar. . . . We strap on our revolvers. Making for the cove. A red moon peers from under a cloud. We put in at a rocky beach, La Playita (at foot of Cajobabo). I'm the last one in the boat, emptying it. Jump ashore. Great joy . . . Up through rocks, thorns, and marshland. Hear noise and get ready, near a fence. Bypassing a farm, we come to a house. We sleep close together, on the ground.[92]

Martí had finally returned to his patria.

THROUGH THE COUNTRYSIDE

Antonio Maceo had already landed in Oriente province and was making his way through rough country to Guantánamo in southeastern Cuba. Maceo had split his force into smaller groups to avoid being discovered. Gómez and Martí met one of these groups and pressed on, hoping to meet Maceo. As they moved through the countryside of eastern Cuba, they picked up volunteers and sympathizers who were willing to join them. They also learned from friendly farmers that the Spanish Army was chasing them. The small invasion force continued westward until it reached the area around Guantánamo. Martí wrote, "For fourteen days I carried my rucksack and rifle on foot across brambles and high places—rousing the people to take up arms as we passed through. . . . The countryside is indisputably ours, to such a degree that in a month I've heard gunfire only once."[93]

On April 16, Gómez surprised Martí by making him a major general of the Cuban Liberation Army. Even though the appointment was just for show, Martí was pleased and proud of the recognition. He wrote in his diary, "Up until today I have never felt that I was a man. I have lived ashamed and have dragged the chain of my fatherland all of my life."[94]

Antonio Maceo was killed in the fight for Cuban independence in 1896. This monument, in Havana, was erected to memorialize Maceo and his contributions to the war.

Yet Martí was still far more important as a writer and propagandist than a fighter. In April, George Bryson, a correspondent for the *New York Herald*, interviewed Martí about his goals for Cuban independence. Martí did not welcome interference by the United States, but he did want to convince the world of the justice of the cause of Cuban independence. The interview with Martí helped create sympathy in the United States for the Cuban revolt.

THE LAST MEETING WITH MACEO

Antonio Maceo was operating in the area around Santiago, the largest city in eastern Cuba. Because of Maceo's reputation, he had managed to attract an army of more than 5,000 volunteers. On May 5, 1895, Martí and Gómez finally linked up with Maceo.

MACEO'S LAST CAMPAIGN

In November 1895, Antonio Maceo launched an amazing invasion of western Cuba. His troops, mostly Afro-Cubans on horseback, covered more than 1,000 miles in three months and fought the Spanish in more than 20 separate battles. With his small army, Maceo unleashed revolutionary war throughout the island. The invasion is one of the most brilliant military feats of the nineteenth century.

Maceo felt that Cubans alone could win their independence from Spain. He wrote, "Liberty is conquered with the edge of the machete, it is not asked for; to beg for one's rights is a device of cowards, incapable of exercising such rights. Nor do I expect any benefit from the Americans; everything must be accomplished through our own efforts; 'tis best to rise or fall without assistance than to contract debts of gratitude with so powerful a neighbor."*

Spanish General Martínez Campos and then General Valeriano Weyler pursued Maceo, fearful that he would spread the revolt and destroy the Cuban sugar industry. On December 7, 1896, the Spanish killed Maceo as he tried to rejoin Gómez's forces. When he died at age 51, Maceo had devoted more than 30 years of his life to fighting for Cuban independence. He had waged hundreds of battles, received 26 bullet wounds, and had lost his father and several brothers in the war.

* Available online at
  http://198.62.75.1/www2/fcf/antonio.maceo.ff.html.

This meeting, held in the La Mejorana sugar mill complex near Santiago, did not go smoothly. The three leaders agreed that they had to spread the revolt to the western part of Cuba as soon as possible. Maceo, however, wanted Martí to return to the United States to organize fund-raising for the revolutionary forces. He did not believe that a poet who had never fought in a war could be useful in Cuba. Martí had contacts in the United States that Maceo wanted him to use. Martí, however, refused to leave. He insisted that he was needed in Cuba.

Maceo and Martí also disagreed on the future of Cuba. Martí wanted the government to be a republic in the hands of elected civilian representatives. Maceo thought this was unrealistic. He believed that a small group of army officers could best steer Cuba through its first difficult years of independence. Martí, of course, could not accept an independent Cuba run by the army. He had spoken against military government almost his entire life. He was not about to compromise now.

The men exchanged some angry words and Maceo cut the meeting short. Although they did not part as friends, Maceo did allow Martí to speak to the troops. Martí promised Maceo's forces that there would be no surrender until Cuba had won its independence. Then Maceo's men rode off.

THE WAR DIARY

Martí, Gómez, and their small force resumed their westward march. On May 12, they made temporary camp at Dos Rios, a small town in the foothills of the Contramaestre Mountains. Martí continued to write letters to various revolutionary groups, made appeals for support to exile groups abroad, and sent personal letters to family, friends, and people in high places.

For the first time in his life, Martí began to keep a regular diary. The first entry, on February 14, 1895, declared that he would write the diary as a link to the teenage daughters of Carmen Miyares. The first part contains very little information about politics. Instead, he filled it with descriptions of people, places, and funny incidents. After Martí reached Cuba on April 11, however, the so-called "war diary" becomes more serious. During his days as a soldier, Martí somehow found the time to write down not only the events of each day but also his hopes for an independent Cuba. Here are some sample excerpts from entries:[95]

> *April 17, 1895*: Morning in camp. Yesterday a cow was slaughtered and as the sun comes up, groups are already standing around the cauldrons. . . . We'll leave tomorrow. I tuck the *Life of Cicero* into the same pocket where I'm carrying 50 bullets. I write letters. The General makes a sweet of coconut shavings with honey. Tomorrow's departure is arranged.

> *April 26*: We form ranks at sunrise. To horse, still sleepy. The men are shaky, haven't yet recovered. They barely ate last night. About 10, we rest along both sides of the path. . . . In the afternoon and at night I write, to New York, to Antonio Maceo who is nearby and unaware of our arrival, and the letter to Manuel Fuentes, to *The World*, which I finished, pencil in hand, at dawn. Yesterday I cast an occasional glance over the calm, happy camp: the sound of a bugle; loads of plantains carried on shoulders; the bellow of the seized cattle when their throats are slit.

> *May 16*: Conversation with Pacheco, the captain: the Cuban people want affection and not despotism; because of despotism many Cubans went over to the government and they'll do it again; what exists in the countryside is a people that has gone out in search of someone to treat it better than the Spaniard, and that thinks it only fair for its sacrifice to be acknowledged.

THE LAST LETTER

On May 17, Gómez learned that a Spanish force was in the area. He left immediately with a large number of men to scout the Spanish and possibly engage them in battle. The general ordered Martí to stay with the rear guard during the fighting.

The next day, Martí wrote from Dos Rios to Manuel Mercado, his friend in Mexico with whom he had kept up a correspondence since 1875. Mercado now had a high position with the Mexican government. Martí had written literally thousands of letters in his lifetime. This would be the last one.

The letter opened, "Every day now I am in danger of giving my life for my country." Martí repeated his dreams of democracy and racial and social harmony for Cuba but he also attacked the United States at some length. Martí wrote that he was fighting mainly to keep Cuba free of outside influences and "to prevent, by the independence of Cuba, the United States from spreading over the West Indies and falling with that added weight upon other lands of our America."

"Our America," of course, was a phrase that Martí used often to refer to Latin America. In his last days, Martí seemed more fearful of the United States than of Spain. He felt that the Cubans would eventually overthrow their colonial masters. He worried, however, that the United States, which he called "the turbulent and brutal North," would take over Cuba and use it as a stepping-stone to dominate all of Latin America.

Some of Martí's fears for Cuba would turn out to be correct, but he would not live to see them realized. His letter to Mercado breaks off in the middle of a sentence as if he had something else to do. It was never finished and never sent.

A MARTYR'S DEATH

On May 19, 1895, the Spanish Army attacked Gómez's forces. The military leaders ordered Martí to stay with the rear guard during the fighting. His life was too valuable to risk in the battle and he had no experience as a soldier.

Martí heard the sounds of gunfire near the Contramaestre River. He could not bear to remain in camp while the others were fighting and dying for a cause that he had promoted his entire life. In March 1895, he had written to his friend Federico

José Martí died in the Battle of Dos Ríos on May 19, 1895. He is now buried in this tomb in the Santa Ifigenia cemetery, in Santiago de Cuba.

Henríquez y Carvajal that he did not want to be a man "who preached the need of dying without beginning by risking his own life. . . . The person who thinks of himself does not love his country. . . . My one desire would be to stay beside the last tree, the last fighter, and die in silence."[96]

Martí refused to wait in the rear. He disobeyed orders by taking a horse and riding out into the battle. As he rode through a pass, he galloped right into the Spanish line of fire and Spanish soldiers shot him dead. He was 42 years old.

Charles Dana, Martí's old friend and editor of the *New York Sun*, wrote that Martí "died as such a man might wish to die, battling for liberty and democracy." The poet Rubén Darío composed a more emotional outburst after hearing of Martí's death:

> Oh, Cuba! You are certainly very beautiful and those of your children that fight for your freedom perform a glorious task . . . but the blood of Martí was not yours alone; it belonged to an entire race, to an entire continent; it belonged to the powerful young that lose in him the first of its teachers; he belongs to the future."[97]

The Spanish buried the body nearby. When they learned that the dead man was José Martí, they dug up the body and carried it to Santiago. On May 27, 1895, Martí was reburied there in the Santa Ifigenia cemetery.

José Martí's Legacy

José Martí's death was a setback for the Cuban independence movement, but it did not end the Cuban revolt. Maceo and Gómez continued fighting, and the rebels won some victories against the Spanish. By 1896, they controlled most of the Cuban countryside while the Spanish still held the large cities. The Spanish Army out-numbered the rebels by about five to one but the morale of Spanish soldiers was low. They were fighting far from home, in terrible con-ditions, for a cause many of them did not believe in. The Spanish sent more than 200,000 soldiers to Cuba, but could not win the war. Martí's death, the crumbling Cuban economy, and Spain's misman-agement all helped spread the Cuban war of independence.

In February 1896, the Spanish replaced the lenient Arsenio Martínez de Campos with General Valeriano Weyler, a tough and ruthless soldier. Weyler organized a brutal "reconcentration" policy. He tried to move the Cuban population in the countryside into prison-like camps to destroy the rebellion's popular support.

97

Cubans died by the thousands in these camps, victims of unsanitary conditions, overcrowding, and disease.

When news of "Butcher" Weyler's policies reached the United States, North American sympathy created a tidal wave of support for the cause of Cuba Libre. Newspapers in the United States filled their pages with stories of Weyler's reconcentration camps. The moral outrage ensured that the Cuban revolt received the full attention of the president and Congress. This was ironic considering that the U.S. Army had used almost the same tactics as Weyler against Native Americans in the West.

In February and April 1896, the U.S. Congress passed resolutions welcoming the future independence of Cuba. Speakers attacked Spain so viciously that anti-United States riots broke out in Spain. President Grover Cleveland issued a proclamation of neutrality, but he also urged Spain to grant the island limited independence. Although many North Americans supported the Cuban war of independence, the dramatic presidential election of 1896 deflected attention in the United States. The issue was not a crisis when William McKinley became president in 1897. McKinley also urged neutrality but he favored the Cuban rebels more than Cleveland did. McKinley protested against Spain's "uncivilized and inhuman" conduct in Cuba.

Late in 1897, a new government in Spain recalled Weyler and agreed to grant the Cubans a form of limited independence. It also declared an amnesty for political prisoners and released North Americans from Cuban jails. Just when a solution seemed possible, Spanish Army officers led riots in Havana on January 12, 1898, against the new Spanish policy. The riots shook McKinley's confidence in Spain's ability to control the situation in Cuba. On January 24, he ordered the battleship *Maine* to Havana, supposedly to protect U.S. citizens but more as a demonstration of U.S. power.

"REMEMBER THE *MAINE*"

At 9:40 on the evening of February 15, 1898, an explosion rocked the *Maine*, killing 266 members of its 354-man crew.

The mysterious explosion of the USS *Maine* on February 15, 1898, helped spur the American people to support war with Spain. "Remember the *Maine*, to hell with Spain" served as a rallying cry for Americans throughout the Spanish-American War.

The actual cause of the *Maine* explosion has never been determined officially. On March 27, 1898, a U.S. investigating board reported that an external explosion caused the sinking of the *Maine*, but "was unable to obtain evidence fixing responsibility . . . upon any person or persons."[98] Most Americans at the time assumed that the culprits were Spanish, although it made no sense for the Spanish to do something to encourage the United States to intervene in Cuba. No credible evidence has ever appeared that any Spaniard, authorized or unauthorized, blew up the ship.

Whatever the cause, war fever swept the United States. On March 27, President McKinley told the Spanish government that it needed to grant a six-month cease-fire to the rebels and close the reconcentration camps or risk a war with the United States. The Spanish government tried to hedge, caught between the fears of revolution at home if it gave in and war abroad if it did not. In April 1898, the Spanish agreed to McKinley's demands to end the fighting and eliminate the reconcentration camps, but McKinley ignored the concessions.

On April 11, 1898, McKinley asked Congress for a declaration of war against Spain. In his speech, a dull 7,000-word message, McKinley declared, "In the name of humanity, in the name of civilization, in behalf of endangered American interests which give us the right and the duty to speak and to act, the war in Cuba must stop."[99] On April 19, Congress passed a joint resolution recognizing the independence of Cuba and authorizing the use of U.S. armed forces to drive out the Spanish. A few days later, Spain declared war on the United States. Congress passed its own declaration of war on April 25, and McKinley signed it the same afternoon.

Crucial to the fate of Cuba was an amendment to the declaration of war proposed by Senator Henry Teller of Colorado. The so-called Teller Amendment promised that the United States would not annex Cuba after the war. The Teller Amendment passed without any opposition. Nothing was said about any other Spanish possessions in the Caribbean (such as Puerto Rico) or the Pacific (like the Philippines) that the United States might want to acquire.

THE SPANISH-AMERICAN WAR

The Spanish-American War lasted only 113 days. It began in April and was over by August. The Spanish Army in Cuba was completely defeated by superior U.S. forces, especially on the sea. John Hay, the U.S. ambassador to Great Britain, called it "a splendid little war." Approximately 5,500 U.S. troops died in the Spanish-American War, but only 379 died in battle. The rest fell victim to a variety of accidents and diseases. About 50,000 Spaniards died in the war, more than 90 percent from disease.

Although the Spanish-American War lasted only 113 days, it led to dramatic changes for Cuba and for relations between Latin America and the United States. Scenes from the war are detailed in this mosaic.

The U.S. entry into the Cuban revolt against Spain meant that the Cubans lost control of their own revolution. When the Spanish surrendered in August 1898, U.S. General William Shafter refused to allow Cuban rebel leaders to participate in the formal surrender. The United States dealt directly with Spain during peace negotiations as though the Cuban Liberation Army did not exist. Novelist Stephen Crane, who covered the war for the *New York World*, reported that U.S. "officers and privates have the most lively contempt for the Cubans. They despise them."[100]

The Treaty of Paris was signed only by the United States and Spanish representatives in December 1898. It granted independence to Cuba and gave the Philippines, Puerto Rico, and Guam to the United States. To soothe Spanish pride, the United States paid $20 million to Spain. By a narrow vote, the U.S. Senate approved the Treaty of Paris on February 6, 1899.

Three years after the death of José Martí, Cuba was free from Spain. General Máximo Gómez expressed the disappointment of the Cuban patriots: "None of us thought that the American intervention would be followed by a military occupation of our country by our allies, who treat us as a people incapable of acting for ourselves. . . . This cannot be our ultimate fate after years of struggle."[99]

LITTLE OR NO INDEPENDENCE

José Martí had said, "Once the United States is in Cuba, who will get her out?"[100] The United States had supposedly fought the war against Spain to free Cuba from Spanish rule. Now, the United States was not willing to let Cuba lead an independent existence. At first, U.S. forces simply remained in Cuba from 1898 to 1902. The new government that Martí dreamed of was never formed. Instead, the United States took over all government and commercial functions. The wealthy landowners regained their old positions in the social and economic order of Cuba. North American corporations were given special privileges. Everything Martí feared about U.S. involvement in Cuba had come to pass.

In 1900, a Cuban constitutional convention met in Havana and drafted a framework for the new Cuban government. The United States pressured the Cubans to accept the so-called Platt Amendment (named after Senator Orville Platt of Connecticut). According to the Platt Amendment, Cuba agreed to make no treaties with foreign powers and permitted the United States to intervene in Cuban affairs. Cuba also agreed to sell or lease lands to the United States for naval bases. In 1903, the United States leased a site in Cuba at Guantánamo Bay for a naval base that grew to cover more than 40 square miles. The Platt Amendment was placed directly in the constitution of Cuba on June 12, 1901. The Cubans reluctantly accepted the Platt Amendment, because it seemed to be the only way to get U.S. soldiers out of Cuba and achieve any degree of Cuban self-government.

Although the U.S. Army left Cuba in 1902, the Platt Amendment allowed the United States to dominate Cuban politics and the economy for the next 30 years. The United States did help build up the Cuban economy and educational system; North Americans built roads, schools, and hospitals. However, as General Leonard Wood wrote to President Theodore Roosevelt, "There is, of course, little or no independence left for Cuba under the Platt Amendment."[101]

In the first half of the 1900s, Cuba was almost a colony of the United States. Several times, the United States sent its own military forces to intervene in Cuban politics. More importantly, the United States used the threat of invasion to allow North American corporations and businesses to take over the Cuban economy. The Platt Amendment was finally removed from the Cuban Constitution after a popular uprising in 1933. However, the United States kept its lease on the naval base at Guantánamo Bay.

FIDEL CASTRO'S REVOLUTION

From 1902 to 1959, the Cuban government seemed to lurch from political chaos to U.S.-supported dictators. The one constant was U.S. control of the Cuban economy and natural resources. In the 1950s, U.S. companies owned more than three-quarters of the mines, ranches, and oil refineries in Cuba and almost half of the sugar industry and the railroads.

Fulgencio Batista ruled Cuba twice during this period, from 1933 to 1944 and from 1952 to 1959. Batista gave the nation a strong government, but he was a dictator who stayed in power by jailing and terrorizing his opponents. Batista also stole large sums of money, making illegal fortunes for himself and his friends. One of the many opponents of Batista was Fidel Castro, who led the rebel forces that toppled Batista's rule. Batista fled Havana to the Dominican Republic, and Castro and his forces entered the city in triumph on January 1, 1959.

When Castro took power, he made major changes to Cuban society. He began a program of radical land reform. He

In 1958, Fidel Castro led a revolt that overthrew the Cuban government. Castro then installed a Communist government and still serves as Cuba's head of state.

allowed the Cuban government to take over leading Cuban industries, even if they were owned by private citizens or controlled by the United States. He began social programs that introduced universal health care and expanded free public education. Soon, the standard of living of the average Cuban was much higher than elsewhere in the Caribbean.

However, Castro was also a dictator. He did not allow any opposing political parties, he limited freedom of speech, and he jailed people who did not agree with him. Many Cubans fled the island for Florida until Castro restricted emigration. Fidel Castro still rules Cuba today. Many people admired him, many despised him, and the judgment of history is still unclear.

CASTRO, MARTÍ, AND THE UNITED STATES

Fidel Castro always claimed to be an admirer of José Martí. Throughout his career, Castro has insisted that he was carrying out Martí's ideals. He did especially follow Martí's warnings about the importance of Cuba remaining independent from the United States. For example, Castro's Cuban government tried to get the United States to give up its military base at Guantánamo Bay on Cuban soil. However, the United States refused to leave.

On the other hand, Castro's critics point out that Castro formed a military dictatorship and a one-party state in Cuba. Martí always hated these forms of government and spoke out against them throughout his life. Therefore, both Castro and his opponents have found something in Martí's message to support their position.

Castro claimed to follow the principles of Karl Marx, a nineteenth-century economist, philosopher, and revolutionary. Martí did write an essay in 1883 entitled, "Tributes to Karl Marx, Who Has Died." In this essay, Martí praised Marx, "for he placed himself on the side of the weak." He also criticized Marx for his attempt to bring about warfare between the rich and the poor: "To set men against men is an appalling task." In truth, however, Martí barely noticed Marx. Outside of this essay, he only mentions Karl Marx twice in the 27 volumes of his collected works.[102]

At first, the U.S. government supported Castro, but then it turned against him. In 1961, the United States encouraged an invasion of Cuba, sometimes known as the Bay of Pigs invasion, by modern-day filibusters. The U.S.-sponsored attack was a complete failure and the invaders were defeated in just three days. After this failure, the U.S. government tried to assassinate Castro. When that did not work, the U.S. government declared

A CUBAN HERO

In the early 1900s, José Martí, much like Antonio Maceo and Máximo Gómez, was a hero for the people of Cuba. His reputation grew after a military coup in 1933, when the people removed the Platt Amendment from the constitution. Martí's name began to be mentioned in speeches, dedications, memorials, and any event in which Cubans took pride in their past. Martí's likeness appeared on postage stamps, coins, medals, and statues. Words were formed from his name. *Martíano* referred to anyone or anything that reflected the ideals of Martí. *Martíanismo* dealt with anything that had to do with Martí. People referred to him as the "Apostle of Cuba," a strange name given Martí's cool feelings toward Christianity.

The problem was that the more Martí's name was mentioned, the less he seemed to stand for. Radicals and reactionaries, conservatives and liberals, all found something in Martí's life or writings to support their own political party or program. In Cuba, Martíanismo was used by anyone who wanted to revolt against the government and by the government itself against popular uprisings. Everyone used Martí's image and interpreted his words for their own purposes.

Today, Martí is loved by Cubans, regardless of how they feel about politics. Since 1959, both those loyal to the Cuban Revolution and those in exile have claimed to believe in Martí's ideals. His fame has especially grown under the rule of Fidel Castro. Havana's airport, library, and central square are all named after Martí. Castro claims that Martí is the true founder of the 1959 Cuban Revolution. At the same time, Cuban exiles and other anti-Castro groups also use Martí's words to attack Castro's dictatorship. The anti-Castro radio station that broadcasts from Florida to Cuba bears the name "Radio Martí."*

---

* John Kirk, *Jose Marti: Mentor of the Cuban Nation* (Gainesville, Fla.: University Press of Florida), ix.

Today, José Martí is still remembered as a popular hero throughout Cuba.
This billboard, in Havana, states—"A virtuous people lives happier"—and
serves to remind Cubans of Martí's great legacy.

an economic boycott (refusal to trade) against Cuba. This
boycott has lasted more than 40 years, despite huge changes in
the political situation over that time.

A CUBAN HERO

Although José Martí died in 1895, he remains a living presence
for almost all Cubans. If nothing else, he stood for tolerance of
other races and beliefs, the right of people and nations to
determine their own future, and a love of literature, art, music,
and learning. More than 100 years after his death, these quali-
ties are still not very common among national leaders. Martí
remains a Cuban hero and an international hero.

Martí set the standard by which he wanted to be judged. In
one letter, he wrote, "Do not say of me, because it is worth little: 'He wrote well, he spoke well.' Say instead, 'He has a sincere

heart, an ardent temperament, he is an honorable man.'" To a large degree, Martí managed to fulfill this description.[103] His final legacy, which no one can dispute, is an independent Cuba. For this cause, he struggled all his life. At the moment of truth, he even sacrificed himself. Martí's memory will live as long as there are people who love Cuba.

Chronology and Timeline

1492	Christopher Columbus lands in Cuba and claims the island for Spain.
1520	First large group of African slaves arrives in Cuba.
1810–30	All of Spain's colonies in the Western Hemisphere gain their independence except Cuba and Puerto Rico.
1850	José Martí's parents move to Cuba.
1851	Narciso Lopez, famous filibuster, captured and executed in Cuba.
1853	José Julián Martí y Pérez born on January 28, in Havana, Cuba.
1865	Martí attends Municipal Senior Boys' School.
1867	Census reveals that Cuba has total population of 1.37 million, of whom 765,000 (56 percent) are considered "white" and 605,000 (44 percent) are "black."
1868	Beginning of the Ten Years' War for Cuban independence.
1869	Writes for underground newspaper; Spanish arrest him and accuse him of treason.
1870	Spanish court sentences Martí to prison for six years; sentence changed to exile.
1871	Martí deported to Spain; enrolls at Central University of Madrid; Spanish execute eight medical students in Cuba in 27 of November incident.
1873	King Amadeus of Spain abdicates; First Spanish Republic created; *Virginius* Affair brings the United States and Cuba to the brink of war; Martí writes the pamphlet *The Political Prison in Cuba*.
1874	Fall of the First Spanish Republic; Martí completes his university education and leaves Spain for Paris.
1875	Arrives in Mexico; lives there happily until rise of dictator Porfirio Díaz.

1876	Leaves Mexico for Cuba.
1877	Arrives in Cuba under a false name; leaves Cuba for Guatemala; appointed professor at Central School of Guatemala; marries Carmen Zayas Barzán.
1878	Ten Years' War for Cuban independence ends in stalemate; Martí's son, José Martí Zayas Bazán, born in November.
1879	Returns to Cuba; outbreak of Little War for Independence of Cuba against Spain; Martí accused of conspiracy and deported.
1880	Arrives in New York City; moves into boardinghouse owned by Manuel Mantilla and his wife, Carmita Miyares de Mantilla; Writes for magazines and newspapers in the United States and Latin America; Little War for Independence crushed; María Mantilla born in November.

1853
José Martí born in Havana, Cuba

1868
Beginning of the Ten Years' War for Cuban independence

1873
Martí writes *The Political Prison in Cuba*

1853   1873

1865
Martí attends Municipal Senior Boys' School

1869
Spanish arrest Martí and accuse him of treason

1881   Teaches briefly in Venezuela; leaves Venezuela and returns to New York.

1882   Publishes *Ismaelillo*, his first book of poems; completes *Versos Libres*.

1884   Resigns from revolutionary movement led by Máximo Gómez; Translates *Ramona* by Helen Hunt Jackson into Spanish.

1885   Manuel Mantilla dies; the area around Tampa becomes a center of the cigar-making industry and Spanish-language culture.

1889   Begins a new children's magazine called *La Edad de Oro*; Martí writes "The Vindication of Cuba."

1890   Writes *Versos Sencillos*; published the next year; U.S. investors hold nearly $50 million worth of property in Cuba.

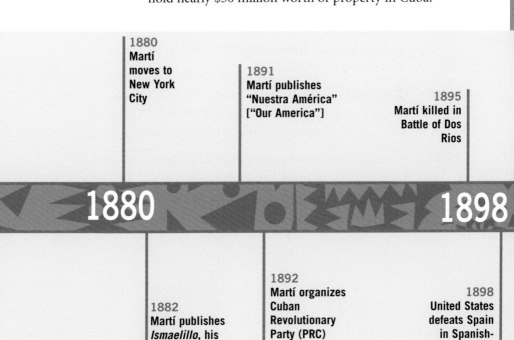

1880
Martí moves to New York City

1891
Martí publishes "Nuestra América" ["Our America"]

1895
Martí killed in Battle of Dos Rios

1880 **1898**

1882
Martí publishes *Ismaelillo*, his first book of poems

1892
Martí organizes Cuban Revolutionary Party (PRC)

1898
United States defeats Spain in Spanish-American War

1891	Publishes "Nuestra América" ["Our America"], his most famous essay; Martí serves as Uruguay's representative to the International Monetary Conference; Makes first visit to Tampa, Florida; writes *Bases of the Cuban Revolutionary Party*.
1892	Forms the Cuban Revolutionary Party [PRC]; Martí edits *La Patria*, a Spanish-language newspaper and official voice of the PRC.
1893	Writes "Mi Raza" ["My Race"].
1894	Organizes the Fernandina Plan to invade and liberate Cuba.
1895	Fernandina Plan fails; PRC gives order for general revolt in Cuba; Martí and Máximo Gómez sign the Manifesto of Montecristi; Martí lands in Cuba [April 11]; killed in Battle of Dos Rios [May 19].
1896	Cuban General Antonio Maceo killed in battle against Spanish; Spanish General Valeriano Weyler begins brutal "reconcentration" policy.
1898	USS *Maine* explosion; United States declares war on Spain; United States defeats Spain in Spanish-American War; United States occupies Cuba until 1904.
1904	Cuban government includes Platt Amendment in Constitution, allowing United States to dictate Cuba's foreign policy.

Notes

Chapter 1

1 John Kirk, *José Martí: Mentor of the Cuban Nation* (Gainesville, Fla.: University Press of Florida, 1983), 24.
2 José Martí, *José Martí, Major Poems: A Bilingual Edition.* Elinor Randall, trans. Philip S. Foner, ed. (New York: Holmes and Meier, 1982), 86–87.
3 José Martí, *Selected Writings.* Esther Allen, ed. and trans. (New York: Penguin, 2002), 295.
4 José Martí, *Versos Sencillos: Simple Verses.* Manuel Tellechea, trans. (Houston, Tex.: Arte Público Press, 1997), XXXIV; Vaughn, 5.
5 *Versos Sencillos*, III.
6 Christopher Abel and Nissa Torrents, eds. *José Martí: Revolutionary Democrat* (Durham, N.C.: Duke University Press, 1986), 118.

Chapter 2

7 Kirk, 23.
8 *Poems*, 1.
9 Kirk, 27.
10 José Martí, *Selected Writings*, 7.
11 Ibid., 8.
12 *Poems*, 125–129.
13 Kirk, 30.
14 Ibid., 40.

Chapter 3

15 David Goodnough, *José Martí: Cuban Patriot and Poet* (Springfield, N.J.: Enslow Publishers, 1996), 32.
16 José Martí, *Versos Sencillos: Simple Verses*, 4.
17 Kirk, 44.
18 José Martí, *Our America* by *José Martí: Writings on Latin America and the Struggle for Cuban Independence.* Elinor Randall, trans. Philip S. Foner, ed. (New York: Monthly Review Press, 1977), 147, 137–47.
19 *Poems*, 4.
20 Ibid.
21 Ibid.
22 José Martí, *Selected Writings*, 256.
23 *Poems*, 74–77.
24 Goodnough, 52.

Chapter 4

25 Available online at *http://www.historyofcuba.com/history/funfacts/CesarRom.htm.*
26 José Martí, *Selected Writings*, 92.
27 Ibid., 416.
28 Ibid., 140.
29 Available online at *http://www.granma.cu/ingles/2005/septiembre/vier9/37Martí.html*
30 Allen, 140–141.
31 Kirk, 119.
32 Ibid., 120–121.
33 Available online at *http://cuba-heritage.com/articles.asp?cID=1&sID=9&ssID=26&offset=175.*
34 José Martí, *Selected Writings*, 258.
35 Kirk, 66.
36 Allen, 259.
37 Foner, *Our America*, 211–215
38 José Martí, *Selected Writings*, 435.

Chapter 5

39 *Poems*, 17.
40 José Martí, *Selected Writings*, 56.
41 Ibid.
42 *Poems*, 56–57.
43 Ibid., 64–65.
44 Ibid., 70–71.
45 José Martí, *Versos Sencillos: Simple Verses*, xx.
46 Ibid., 89.
47 *Poems*, 58–59.
48 Ibid., 122–123.

49 Ibid., 62–63.
50 José Martí, *Selected Writings*, 184, 187, 192.
51 José Martí, *The America of José Martí: Selected Writings*, Juan de Onís, trans. (New York: Noonday Press, 1955), 119, 129.
52 Ibid., 119.

Chapter 6
53 Ibid., 32–33.
54 *The America of José Martí*, 107, 109.
55 Available online at *http://www.historyofcuba.com/history/Martí 4b.htm*.
56 Kirk, 52.
57 Ibid., 50.
58 Abel, 109.
59 José Martí, *Selected Writings*, 35.
60 Ibid., 35.
61 Ibid., 310.
62 Abel, 10.
63 Available online at *http://www.historyofcuba.com/history/Martí 4b.htm*.
64 José Martí, *Selected Writings*, 261–267.
65 Kirk, 51.
66 José Martí, *Selected Writings*, 290.
67 Ibid., 288–296.
68 Available online at *http://www.cubaminrex.cu/jose Martí /jose%20Martí%20vers% 20ingles/Martímonetary%20 conference.htm*.
69 José Martí, *Selected Writings*, 261–267.
70 Ibid., 261–267.

Chapter 7
71 Available online at *http://www.oah.org/pubs/ magazine/1898/mormino.pdf*.

72 Available online at *http://www.ybor.org/historic-clubs/union.asp*.
73 Available online at *http://www.historical-museum.org/history/war/cf.htm*.
74 Foner, *Our America*, 208.
75 Jeffrey Belnap and Raul Fernandez, eds. *José Martí's Our America*: From *National to Hemispheric Cultural Studies* (Durham, N.C.: Duke University Press, 1999), 101.
76 José Martí, *Selected Writings*, 318.
77 Available online at *http://news.tbo.com/news/ MGBDOZ9COVD.html*.
78 Available online at *http://www.spanamwar.com/ Martí.htm*.
79 Available online at *http://www.historical-museum.org/history/war/cf.htm*.
80 Abel, 11.
81 Available online at *http://cuba-heritage.org/articles.asp?11D=12a +ID=206*.
82 Available online at *http://www.oah.org/pubs/maga-zine/1898/mormino.pdf*.

Chapter 8
83 José Martí, *Selected Writings*, 338, 340.
84 Abel, 13.
85 José Martí, *Selected Writings*, 337.
86 Goodnough, 82.
87 José Martí, *Selected Writings*, 335.
88 Ibid., 346.
89 Martí, *On Art and Literature*, 329–333.
90 Belnap, 321.
91 *Poems*, 13–14.
92 Allen, 380.

93 José Martí, *Selected Writings*, 348.
94 Goodnough, 87.
95 José Martí, *Selected Writings*, 350–413.
96 Onís, 313–316.
97 José Martí, *José Martí Reader: Writings on the Americas* (New York: Ocean Books, 2006).

Chapter 9

98 *American Presidents in World History*, vol. 3 (Westport, Conn.: Greenwood Press, 2003), 84.

 99 Ibid., 86.
100 Available online at *http://www.fiu.edu/~fcf/rooseveltsbull.html*
101 Abel, 1
102 Available online at *http://www.eiu.edu/~historia/2003/cuba.htm.*
103 José Martí, *Selected Writings*, 130–139.
104 Abel, 113.
105 *Poems*, 94–95.

Bibliography

Abel, Christopher, and Nissa Torrents, eds. *José Martí: Revolutionary Democrat*. Durham, N.C.: Duke University Press, 1986.

Belnap, Jeffrey, and Raul Fernandez, eds. *José Martí's "Our America": From National to Hemispheric Cultural Studies*. Durham, N.C.: Duke University Press, 1999.

Garcia, Cristina, ed. *Cubanisimo! The Vintage Book of Contemporary Cuban Literature*. New York: Vintage, 2003.

Gleiter, Jan. *Jose Marti*. Milwaukee, Wisc.: Raintree, 1988.

Goldman, Francisco. *The Divine Husband: A Novel*. New York: Atlantic Monthly, 2004.

Goodnough, David. *José Martí: Cuban Patriot and Poet*. Springfield, N.J.: Enslow Publishers, 1996.

Gracia, Jorge, and Mireya Camurati, eds. *Philosophy and Literature in Latin America: A Critical Assessment of the Current Situation*. Albany: State University of New York Press, 1989.

Kirk, John. *José Martí: Mentor of the Cuban Nation*. Gainesville, Fla.: University Press of Florida, 1983.

Marinello, Juan. *José Martí*. Madrid: Jucar, 1976.

Martí, José. *The America of José Martí: Selected Writings*. Juan de Onís, trans. New York: Noonday Press, 1953.

Martí, José. *José Martí, Major Poems: A Bilingual Edition*. Elinor Randall, trans. Philip S. Foner, ed. New York: Holmes and Meier, 1982.

———. *Obra Literaria*. Caracas: Biblioteca Ayacucho, 1978.

———. *On Art and Literature by José Martí: Critical Writings*. Elinor Randall, trans. Philip S. Foner, ed. New York: Monthly Review Press, 1982.

———. *Our America by José Martí: Writings on Latin America and the Struggle for Cuban Independence*. Elinor Randall, Philip S. Foner, ed. New York: Monthly Review Press, 1977.

———. *Selected Writings*. Esther Allen, ed. and trans. New York; Penguin Books, 2002.

———. *Versos Sencillos: Simple Verses.* Manuel Tellechea, trans. Houston, Tex.: Arte Público Press, 1997.

———. *Versos Sencillos.* La Habana: Ediciones "La Tertulia," 1961.

Perez, Louis. *José Martí in the United States: The Florida Experience.* Tempe: Arizona State University Press, 1995.

Rodríguez, Julio, ed. *Re-Reading José Martí (1853–1895): One Hundred Years Later.* Albany: State University of New York Press, 1999.

Schulman, Ivan. *Símbolo y Color en la Obra de José Martí.* Madrid: Editorial Gredos, 1970.

Web sites

History of Cuba
http://www.historyofcuba.com/main/hstintro.htm

José Martí: Su Vida y Obra.
http://www.josemarti.org/

José Julián Martí: Cuba's Greatest Hero, Poet, Statesman
http://members.aol.com/josemarticuba/index1.html

Further Reading

Appel, Todd. *José Martí*. New York: Chelsea House, 1992.

Goodnough, David. *José Martí: Cuban Patriot and Poet*. Springfield, N.J.: Enslow Publishers, 1996.

Martí, José. *Jose Marti, Major Poems: A Bilingual Edition*. Elinor Randall, trans. Philip S. Foner, ed. New York: Holmes and Meier, 1982.

———. *Selected Writings*. Esther Allen, ed. and trans. New York: Penguin Books, 2002.

Sherrow, Victoria. *Cuba*. Brookfield, Conn.: Twenty-first Century Books, 2001.

West, Alan. *José Martí: Man of Poetry, Soldier of Freedom*. Brookfield, Conn.: Millbrook, 1994.

Web sites

Cuba's Freedom Fighter: Antonio Maceo (1845–1896)
http://198.62.75.1/www2/fcf/antonio.maceo.ff.html

History of Cuba
http://www.historyofcuba.com/cuba.htm

José Julián Martí: Poetry, Literature, Letters.
http://members.aol.com/enriques/index2.html

José Julián Martí: Cuba's Greatest Hero, Poet, Statesman.
http://members.aol.com/josemarticuba/index1.html

Crucible of Empire: The Spanish-American War
http://www.pbs.org/crucible/

Index

About the Author

Jon Sterngass is the author of *First Resorts: Pursuing Pleasure at Saratoga Springs, Newport, and Coney Island.* He currently is a freelance writer specializing in children's nonfiction books; his most recent work for Chelsea House is *Filipino Americans* in the series THE NEW IMMIGRANTS. Born and raised in Brooklyn, Sterngass has a B.A. in history and philosophy from Franklin and Marshall College, an M.A. from the University of Wisconsin-Milwaukee in medieval history, and a Ph.D., from City University of New York in American history.

Picture Credits